ULTIMATE GUIDE TO PRO HOCKEY TEAMS 2015

by Shane Frederick,
Luke DeCock, and
Martin Gitlin

capstone young readers

Sports Illustrated Kids The Ultimate Guide to Pro Hockey Teams 2015 is published by Capstone Young Readers, 1710 Roe Crest Drive, North Mankato, MN 56003. www.capstonepub.com

Library of Congress Cataloging-in-Publication Data
Cataloging-in-publication information is on file with the Library of Congress.
ISBN 978-1-4914-1963-2

Edited by Clare Lewis and Anthony Wacholtz
Designed by Richard Parker and Eric Manske
Media Research by Eric Gohl
Production by Helen McCreath

Image Credits:
AP Photo: 74, A.E. Maloof, 29, Tom Pidgeon, 101; BigStockPhoto.com: Christopher Penler, 80t; Corbis: Bettmann, 26, 52, 56, 68, 71, 82, 85; Getty Images: Allsport/Robert Laberge, 91, Bruce Bennett Studios, 6, 17, 31t, 50, 69, 72, 73, 83, 89, 100, 103, Focus On Sport, 37t, 58, 90, Hulton Archive, 112, NHL Images/Allsport/Glenn Cratty, 61b, NY Daily News Archive/ Keith Torrie, 19, Pictorial Parade, 113; iStockphotos: Mark Stay, 120–121, Stefan Klein, 120 (puck); Newscom: 87b, 97t, 109t, AFP/Dan Levine, 107b, Icon SMI/Jason Cohn, 117t, Icon SMI/Jason Mowry, 45t, Icon SMI/Robert Beck, 59, Icon SMI/Shelly Castellano, 33b, Icon SMI/Southcreek Sports/ Adrian Gauthier, 110b, Images Distribution, 111b, Reuters/Gary Caskey, 40, Reuters/Mike Segar, 43, Reuters/STR, 8, UPI Photo/John Dickerson, 61t, Zuma Press/The Sporting News, 37b; Sports Illustrated: Bob Rosato, 86b, 108t, 108b, 111t, 119b, Damian Strohmeyer, 24t, 79t, 93t, 98b, 110t, 118b, 123, David E. Klutho, cover, 1, 4–5, 7, 9, 20, 22t, 22b, 23t, 23b, 24b, 30t, 30b, 31b, 32t, 32b, 33t, 34t, 34b, 35b, 36t, 36b, 38t, 38b, 39t, 39b, 42, 44t, 44b, 45b, 46t, 46b, 47b, 48t, 49t, 49b, 54t, 54b, 55b, 60t, 60b, 62b, 63t, 64t, 64b, 65t, 65b, 66t, 76t, 76b, 77t, 77b, 78t, 78b, 79b, 92t, 92b, 93b, 94t, 94b, 96t, 98t, 99t, 99b, 104t, 104b, 109b, 114t, 114b, 115t, 115b, 118t, Heinz Kluetmeier, 15, Hy Peskin, 10, 11, 48b, 51, 66b, 67b, John D. Hanlon, 25b, 28, 95t, 95b, John G. Zimmerman, 86t, John Iacono, 13, 80b, John W. McDonough, 62t, Manny Millan, 12, 35t, 81t, 81b, Robert Beck, 21, 47t, 63b, 96b, 97b, 105t, 105b, 106t, 106b, 107t, 116b, 117b, 122, Simon Bruty, 116t, 119t, Tony Triolo, 2, 25t, 55t, 67t, V.J. Lovero, 87t

Design Elements: iStockphotos, Shutterstock

Printed in Canada.
092014 007105

TABLE OF CONTENTS

THE GREATEST SHOW ON ICE

From its origins on the frozen ponds of Canada to the crowded arenas of today, the game of hockey has always had many loyal fans who cheer every goal, assist, and crunching body check. Hockey is now popular from coast to coast and all the way from Canada to the southern United States. Fans now pack huge arenas every year to cheer for their favorite team.

Today, professional hockey is a much faster and bigger sport than it once was. The NHL now has 30 teams, which this book will explore in detail, looking at both the history and the present-day achievements of each team.

A RICH HISTORY

But as much as fans enjoy the excitement of watching a game, they also enjoy being part of a game that has a century of history. For many years, there were only six teams in the National Hockey League (NHL). These teams are known as the "Original Six" (see the box). It was a slower and rougher game then, but it was full of stories.

The Original Six

The "Original Six" teams in the NHL were the Boston Bruins, Chicago Black Hawks, Detroit Red Wings, Montreal Canadiens, New York Rangers, and Toronto Maple Leafs.

GREAT TEAMS AND STARS

This book also features in-depth looks at some of hockey's greatest individual championship teams and stars. Gordie Howe, Wayne Gretzky, Mario Lemieux, and Bobby Orr, the four greatest players in hockey history, all played on championship teams. New stars are also leading great teams today.

THE STANLEY CUP

The Stanley Cup is the oldest and most famous trophy in professional sports. It has become the symbol of the NHL. Each season, every team sets a goal of winning the Cup.

THE HISTORY OF THE CUP

In 1893 the Montreal Amateur Athletics Association captured the Amateur Hockey Association's championship. Its prize for winning was a $50 silver bowl donated by Sir Frederick Arthur Stanley, the governor general of Canada.

The Montreal Amateur Athletics Association won the first Stanley Cup title in 1893.

After this, the Cup became the trophy teams played for in the "Challenge Cup Era." From 1893 to 1913, Canadian hockey clubs challenged each other to determine the Stanley Cup champion.

Then, from 1914 to 1917, the champions of the Pacific Coast Hockey Association (PCHA) and National Hockey Association (NHA) played for the Stanley Cup. But during these years, many of the NHA's top players left to fight in World War I (1914–1918). With a lack of quality players, the NHA broke apart in 1917.

Several NHA franchise owners soon formed the NHL. The league named the annual championship the Stanley Cup finals. The Cup itself became the prize for winning the title. And today, it keeps getting bigger. More rings are added to the base of the Cup as it is filled with the names of winning players each year.

Winning the Stanley Cup is always cause for great celebration!

THE NHL SEASON AND PLAYOFFS

Today, each of the 30 NHL teams starts each season with the dream of winning the Stanley Cup. The teams are split into the Eastern Conference and Western Conference. Each conference has two divisions of seven or eight teams. Teams play 82 games during the regular season. They receive two points for each victory. If they lose, they get zero points. If a team loses in overtime or in a shootout loss, they receive one point. Overtimes and shootouts are played when teams end three regular periods of play in a tie.

The top eight teams in each conference reach the playoffs. The top three teams from each division advance to the post-season, as do the conference's next two best teams, called wild card teams.

Each playoff round consists of a best-of-seven series. The teams battle through three rounds of playoffs to determine the Eastern and Western Conference winners. The conference champions then play each other in the Stanley Cup finals. The first team to win four games in the finals series is declared the NHL champion.

Fun with the Cup

After the Stanley Cup finals, each player from the winning team gets to keep the Cup for one day during the offseason. The trophy has been on boat rides, in parades, and at parties all around the world! Over the years the Cup has been used as everything from a flowerpot to a soup bowl. It has been used to baptize babies. And some players have allowed their pets to drink out of it!

During a trip to his home country of Slovakia, Detroit's Tomas Kopecky ate tripe soup out of the Stanley Cup!

MOLSON CANADIAN
GOLD STAR MORTGAGE POWER PLAY
The Detroit News

GREATEST DYNASTIES

Throughout Stanley Cup history, several teams have been powerhouses. They've played in many championship series and have come away with several titles. But a few teams have risen even higher to become true dynasties in the league. (For more on these individual teams, read their chapters and "Great Teams in Focus" panels throughout this book.)

Most Stanley Cup Championships

Team	Championships
Montreal Canadiens	24
Toronto Maple Leafs	13
Detroit Red Wings	11
Boston Bruins	6
Edmonton Oilers	5

Montreal Canadiens wing Maurice "Rocket" Richard

CANADA IN COMMAND

From 1942 through most of the 1960s, the Stanley Cup rarely traveled outside of Canada. The Montreal Canadiens and Toronto Maple Leafs dominated the Cup. The Canadiens won 18 titles from 1944 to 1979.

During those 36 seasons, Montreal reached the finals an amazing 24 times. When the Canadiens didn't win the Stanley Cup, the Maple Leafs usually did. The team captured 6 out of 10 titles from 1942 to 1951. Toronto went on to win four more championships between 1962 and 1967.

Montreal Canadiens goalie Gerry McNeil

Montreal Canadiens defenseman Emile "Butch" Bouchard

SUPER ISLANDERS

The NHL began adding teams and expanded rapidly in the late 1960s. It soon became nearly impossible for one team to dominate the Stanley Cup. One exception was the New York Islanders, the first U.S. team to enjoy a dynasty.

The Islanders first entered the league in 1972. They snagged their first Stanley Cup just eight years later, in 1980. The team went on to win three more championships from 1981 to 1983.

The Islanders featured several future NHL Hall of Famers, including Mike Bossy and Bryan Trottier. During their four-year dynasty, the Islanders compiled an incredible 16–3 record in the Stanley Cup finals. During the 1982 and 1983 finals, they never lost a game.

The defensive play of wing Bob Nystrom (opposite) and offensive skills of center Bryan Trottier were key parts of the New York Islanders' championship years.

OVERPOWERING OILERS

The Islanders' dynasty ended just as the Edmonton Oilers began their own. Some believe the Oilers were the most explosive team in NHL history. The team began showing their dominance in 1984. They overpowered their opponents while averaging a league-record 5.58 goals per game. They won the Stanley Cup that year, and again in 1985, 1987, 1988, and 1990.

The Oilers didn't just steamroll through the regular season and playoffs every year. They dominated the championship round, too. With superstar center Wayne Gretzky leading the way, the Oilers scored an average of 21 goals in all five Stanley Cup titles.

The Oilers defense was also dominant during the team's championship years. Opponents averaged just 2.4 goals per game in those series. In the 1990 finals, the Oilers held the Boston Bruins to just eight goals in five games.

Most Points Scored in a Stanley Cup Final Series

Points	Player, Team	Opponent	Year
13	Wayne Gretzky, Oilers	Bruins	1988
12	Gordie Howe, Red Wings	Canadiens	1955
12	Yvan Cournoyer, Canadiens	Blackhawks	1973
12	Jacques Lemaire, Canadiens	Blackhawks	1973
12	Mario Lemieux, Penguins	North Stars	1991

Wayne Gretzky won the 1985 Stanley Cup Most Valuable Player (MVP) award while leading Edmonton to its second championship.

AMAZING MOMENTS

The Stanley Cup finals are often filled with excitement and drama. Over the years the finals have had some historic moments.

1987: EDMONTON VS. PHILADELPHIA

In the 1986–1987 season, the Philadelphia Flyers had the second-best defense in the NHL. The Edmonton Oilers had the NHL's finest offense. It was only a matter of time before the two teams battled for the Stanley Cup championship.

Edmonton won three of the first four games, and Oilers fans were already boasting about a victory parade. But the Flyers showed their talent and guts. The team fell behind by two goals in both Games 5 and 6. But they stormed back to win both games and force a Game 7.

However, Edmonton proved to be too strong of a team. Goaltender Grant Fuhr shut down the Flyers in a 3–1 victory in Game 7. The Oilers won their third championship in four years, and the fans got to enjoy their victory parade.

The Oilers' Mark Messier (left) and the Flyers' Dave Poulin battled to control the puck during Game 3 of the 1987 Stanley Cup finals.

1942: TORONTO VS. DETROIT

The Toronto Maple Leafs appeared doomed in the 1942 Stanley Cup finals. They lost the first two games at home against the Detroit Red Wings. Then they lost Game 3 in Detroit as well.

Toronto coach Hap Day decided to take drastic action. He benched several veteran players and replaced them with rookies. Led by future Hall of Famer Syl Apps, the Leafs responded with three straight wins to force the first Game 7 in Stanley Cup history. In the final game, Toronto's goaltender Turk Broda kept the Red Wings to just one goal. The Leafs won the final game 3–1, achieving possibly the greatest comeback in NHL history.

1994: VANCOUVER VS. NEW YORK

The last time the New York Rangers had won the Stanley Cup, the NHL had just six teams. But the Rangers' fortunes were about to change in the 1994 Stanley Cup finals. The Rangers won three of the first four games against the Vancouver Canucks. New York was on the brink of winning its first championship in 54 years. But the Canucks stormed back to tie the series.

Game 7 and the title were decided at Madison Square Garden in front of nearly 20,000 fans. The fans would not go home disappointed. Star forward Mark Messier scored a goal and an assist to lead the Rangers to a 3–2 victory. After more than 50 years, the Rangers had finally captured another Stanley Cup title. (For more on this amazing championship battle, see pages 88 to 91.)

New York fans celebrated the Rangers' Stanley Cup title with a ticker-tape parade.

LOPSIDED SHOCKER

The Vancouver Canucks were expected to win it all in 2011. The team had the most explosive offense and the strongest defense in the NHL. Vancouver had won 8 of 11 games leading up to the championship round.

But the Canucks seemed outmatched by Boston in the 2011 Stanley Cup series. Vancouver earned a narrow 1–0 victory in the first game of the series. Game 2 went to overtime, which the Canucks also won 3–2.

But then the Bruins turned up the heat. Boston's offense exploded to score 21 goals over the five games and claim the title. Meanwhile, the Canucks managed to score only four goals. Although they were favored to win the championship, Vancouver couldn't overcome Boston's powerful offense.

Boston finished the series with 15 more goals than Vancouver. The Canucks set a record low by scoring just eight goals in seven games. It was the most lopsided score ever seen in a seven-game Stanley Cup series.

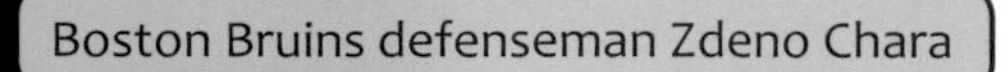
Boston Bruins defenseman Zdeno Chara

Boston Bruins wing Michael Ryder

Vancouver Canucks goalie Roberto Luongo

ANAHEIM DUCKS

First Season: 1993–1994

Franchise Record: 722–637–107–108
Home Rink: Honda Center
(17,174 capacity) in Anaheim, California

STANLEY CUP
2007

The Anaheim Ducks were all Hollywood when they joined the NHL. They were owned by the Walt Disney Company. They got their name—then called the Mighty Ducks of Anaheim—from a popular Disney hockey movie. The goalie even wore a mask that featured the face of cartoon character Donald Duck. But they are no joke. The Ducks have twice gone to the Stanley Cup finals and won it all in 2007.

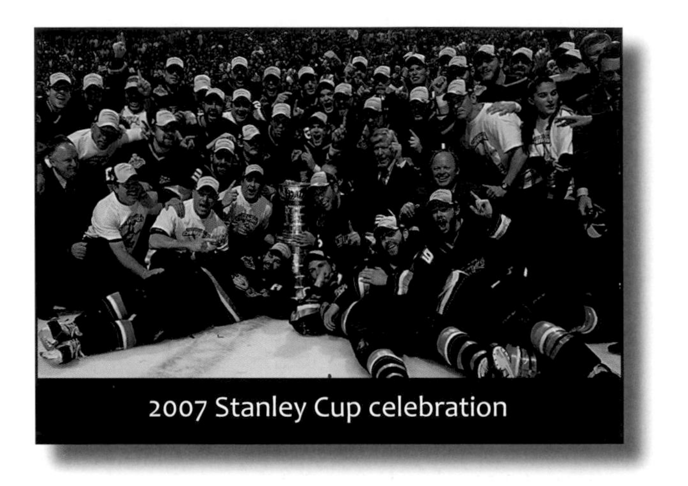

2007 Stanley Cup celebration

Franchise records are listed by wins, losses, ties, and overtime losses.

Legends & Stars

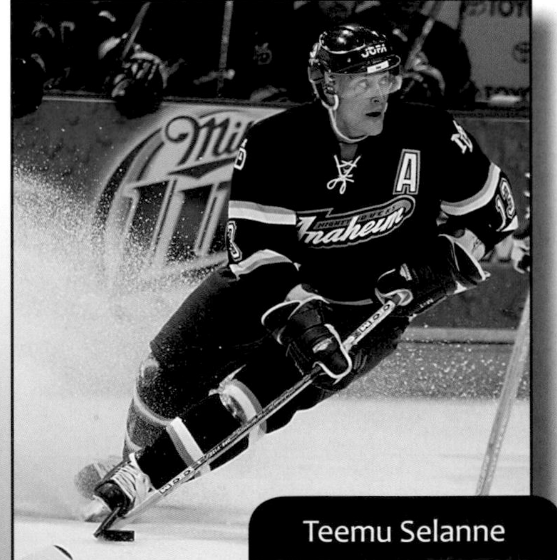

Teemu Selanne

Player	Position	Years	Notes
Paul Kariya	LW	1994–2003	Two-time Lady Byng Trophy winner
Scott Niedermayer	D	2005–2010	Longtime New Jersey Devil was a Conn Smythe winner with the Ducks
Corey Perry	RW	2005–2014	Led NHL in goals and won Hart Trophy in 2011
Teemu Selanne	RW	1996–2001, 2005–2014	NHL's goal leader in 1999 has played in 10 All-Star Games

By the Numbers

TOP GOAL SCORER
Teemu Selanne
1996–2001,
2005–2014
448 goals

TOP GOALTENDER
Jean-Sebastien Giguere
2000–2010
206 wins

TOP ASSISTS MAN
Teemu Selanne
457 goals
531 assists

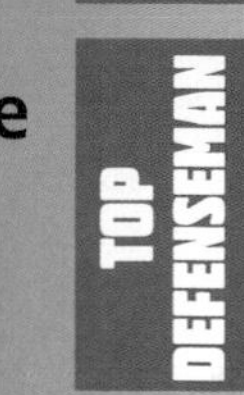

TOP DEFENSEMAN
Scott Niedermayer
2005–2010
264 points

All regular season stats are through the 2013–14 season.

Consolation Prize

The Conn Smythe Trophy is awarded to the MVP of the Stanley Cup playoffs every year. A player on the losing team of the finals has won the award only five times in NHL history. Ducks goaltender Jean-Sebastien Giguere was one of those players. Although the Ducks fell to the Devils in Game 7 of the 2003 finals, Giguere's five shutouts in the playoffs earned him the award.

Rob (left) and Scott Niedermayer

Sibling Rivalry

Rob Niedermayer watched his older brother, Scott, lift the Stanley Cup with the New Jersey Devils three times. Rob never touched the trophy until Scott joined him on the Ducks. They won a title together in 2007.

ARIZONA COYOTES

Franchise Record: 1,121–1,206–266–105

Home Rink: Jobing.com Arena (17,653 capacity) in Glendale, Arizona

STANLEY CUPS

None

First Season: 1979–1980

In 1979 the four remaining World Hockey Association (WHA) teams merged into the NHL. One of those was the Winnipeg Jets, a three-time WHA champion led by former NHL superstar Bobby Hull. The Jets were the WHA's last title winner. The team played 17 seasons in Manitoba, Canada, before leaving in 1996 for the American desert and becoming the Phoenix, and later Arizona, Coyotes.

Coyotes right wing Shane Doan was selected to two All-Star Games.

Legends & Stars

Jeremy Roenick

Shane Doan	RW	1995–present	Original Coyote played in two All-Star Games
Dale Hawerchuk	C	1981–1990	1982 Calder Trophy winner played nine seasons with the Jets
Teppo Numminen	D	1988–2003	Three-time All-Star selection played 15 seasons with the Jets/Coyotes
Jeremy Roenick	C	1996–2001, 2006–2007	Nine-time All-Star Game selection
Keith Tkachuk	LW	1991–2001	Five-time All-Star pick played in Winnipeg and Phoenix

By the Numbers

Dale Hawerchuk
1981–1990
379 goals

Ilya Bryzgalov
2007–2011
130 wins

Thomas Steen
1981–1995
553 assists

Teppo Numminen →
1988–2003
534 points

Zero Tolerance

In 2004 Coyotes goaltender Brian Boucher broke what many thought would be an untouchable record. He set the modern record for consecutive shutouts, blanking teams in five straight games. He kept the puck out of his goal for 332 minutes, 1 second.

Gretzky Joins the Team

Wayne Gretzky played for the Oilers, Kings, Blues, and Rangers. He took on a different role with the Coyotes, becoming a partial owner in 2000. He was also put in charge of managing the hockey team. In 2005 he named himself the team's head coach. Gretzky coached for four seasons, winning 143 games.

Franchise Record: 2,938–2,240–791–121

Home Rink: TD Garden
(17,565 capacity) in Boston, Massachusetts

STANLEY CUPS
1929, 1939, 1941, 1970, 1972, 2011

First Season: 1924–1925

The Boston Bruins were the first American team to join the Canadian-born NHL. Over their nearly 90 seasons, the Bs have captured six Stanley Cups. One of the best players to ever lace up the skates was a Boston Bruin: the game-changing defenseman Bobby Orr (see page 30).

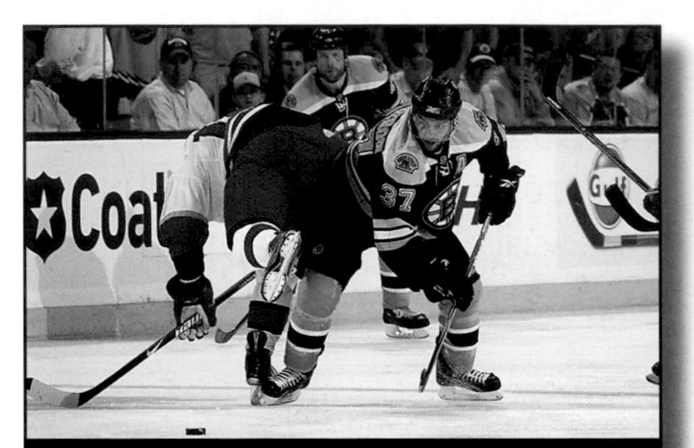
Patrice Bergeron fights for the puck in the 2009 Eastern Conference semifinals.

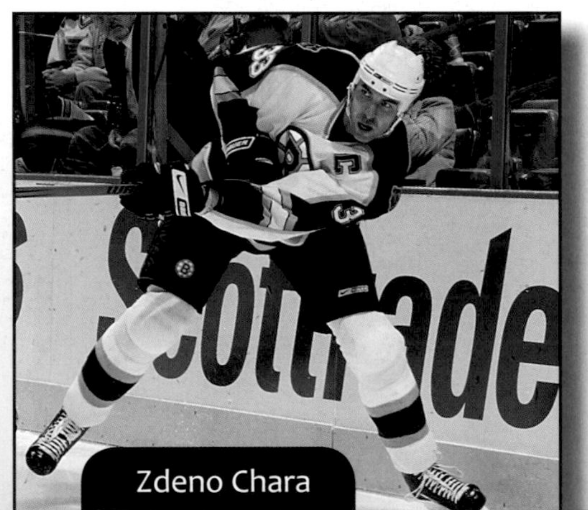
Zdeno Chara

Ray Bourque	D	1979–2000	Bruins all-time points leader with 1,506
Frank Brimsek	G	1938–1943, 1945–1949	"Mr. Zero" had 10 shutouts as a rookie; won two Cups
John Bucyk	LW	1957–1978	Played 21 seasons for the Bruins
Zdeno Chara	D	2006–present	Norris Trophy winner is the tallest player in the NHL
Phil Esposito	C	1967–1975	Led the league in scoring five times
Cam Neely	RW	1986–1996	Named to five All-Star Games
Bobby Orr	D	1966–1976	Won eight Norris, three Hart, and two Conn Smythe trophies
Art Ross		1924–1928, 1929–1934, 1936–1939, 1941–1945	Coached 16 seasons, winning 361 games and the 1939 Stanley Cup
Eddie Shore	D	1926–1939	Four-time Hart Trophy winner
Tim Thomas	G	2002–2012	Won the Vezina and Jennings trophies in 2009

By the Numbers

TOP GOAL SCORER	**John Bucyk** 1957–1978 545 goals	TOP GOALTENDER	**Tiny Thompson** 1928–1938 252 wins
TOP ASSISTS MAN	**Ray Bourque** 1979–2000 1,111 assists	TOP DEFENSEMAN	**Ray Bourque** 1,506 points

Daring Defensemen

Defensemen don't always get the glory—unless they're playing for Boston. The Bruins have had some of the best defensemen to ever play the game. Bobby Orr is considered the best of all time. Eddie Shore was a star in the sport's early days and won four MVPs. Ray Bourque is the top-scoring defenseman of all time.

Bobby Orr (4) in the 1974 NHL playoffs

Breaking Down Barriers

On January 18, 1958, history was made when Bruins winger Willie O'Ree took the ice. O'Ree was the first black player to participate in an NHL game. The Fredericton, New Brunswick, Canada, native had a short professional career. He played in just two games that season and 43 games in 1960–1961. He scored four goals in 1958.

1969-1970 BOSTON BRUINS

Bobby Orr was one of the most talented players in hockey history. His greatest moment was scoring the game-winning goal for the 1970 Stanley Cup, and the 1969–1970 Boston Bruins were the best team he played on.

Bobby Orr and Phil Esposito receive awards for their achievements in the 1969–1970 season.

HISTORY BOX

GROWING THE GAME

The Bruins rose to the top of the NHL at an exciting time for the league. For 24 years, the league had consisted of six teams that had been around since 1926 (see page 4). But for the 1967–1968 season, the NHL expanded to Philadelphia, Los Angeles, St. Louis, Minnesota, Pittsburgh, and Oakland. Other professional sports had added teams before. For hockey, this addition was the first step in becoming a major sport. By 2000 the league had grown from 6 to 30 teams.

1969–1970 Record

Won	Lost	Tied	Playoffs
40	17	19	Defeated New York Rangers 4–2
			Defeated Chicago Blackhawks 4–0
			Defeated St. Louis Blues 4–0

The Bruins won the Cup in 1970 partly thanks to Orr, and partly thanks to a high-scoring center named Phil Esposito. The Bruins had traded for Esposito in 1967. Esposito, then 25 years old, scored 21 goals and 40 assists to finish seventh in the NHL that season. The following season, in 1968–1969, Esposito continued his great offensive play. He became the first player in the league to score more than 100 points. Once he got to Boston, Esposito finished either first or second in scoring in each of the next eight seasons. Behind Esposito and Orr, the Bruins were an unstoppable team.

On the defensive end, the Bruins were very tough. The goalie, Gerry Cheevers, was a colorful character. He painted stitches on his goalie mask to show where pucks had hit him. Orr's defensive play was also changing the game of hockey. Before Orr, defensemen didn't try to score. But Orr liked to skate with the puck and pass. He set up goals like no one else before him. Orr showed that defensemen could do more than just defend. He was the first, and only, defenseman to win a scoring title, with 120 points in 1969–1970. That year, Orr also set an NHL record for 87 assists. He could score, pass, and defend, and this made him one of the game's great players.

During the regular season, the Bruins played in the Eastern Division, which was a very close division. Only seven points separated the first- through fifth-place teams. Meanwhile, the Western Division was very different. The St. Louis Blues won, winning their division by 18 points.

The Blues and the Bruins met in the Stanley Cup finals. In the first game, the Bruins came out strong, scoring an amazing four goals in the third period for an easy 6–1 victory over St. Louis. John Bucyk led Boston, and he scored a hat trick (three goals) for his team, with a goal coming in each period. In Game 2, Boston once again showed they were the better team by scoring six goals. They won the game 6–2.

In Game 3, St. Louis showed they weren't going to back down as they took an early lead. The Bruins fought back behind goals from Bucyk and John McKenzie, and the team took a small 2–1 lead in the third period. In the last period, it was Boston's game, as Wayne Cashman scored two goals to give the Bruins a 4–1 victory and a 3–0 series lead. They were now only one game away from a sweep and winning the Stanley Cup.

Bobby Orr (1948-)

Bobby Orr's jersey number—No. 4—is retired in Boston, and he is also honored everywhere that hockey is played. With his skating and skills, he created a new role for defensemen. For Orr, scoring goals was as important as stopping the other team from scoring them. He won three straight Hart trophies as the league's MVP and eight straight Norris trophies as its best defenseman. A bad knee forced him to retire in 1978, after only eight seasons. Orr remains one of the game's greatest players of all time.

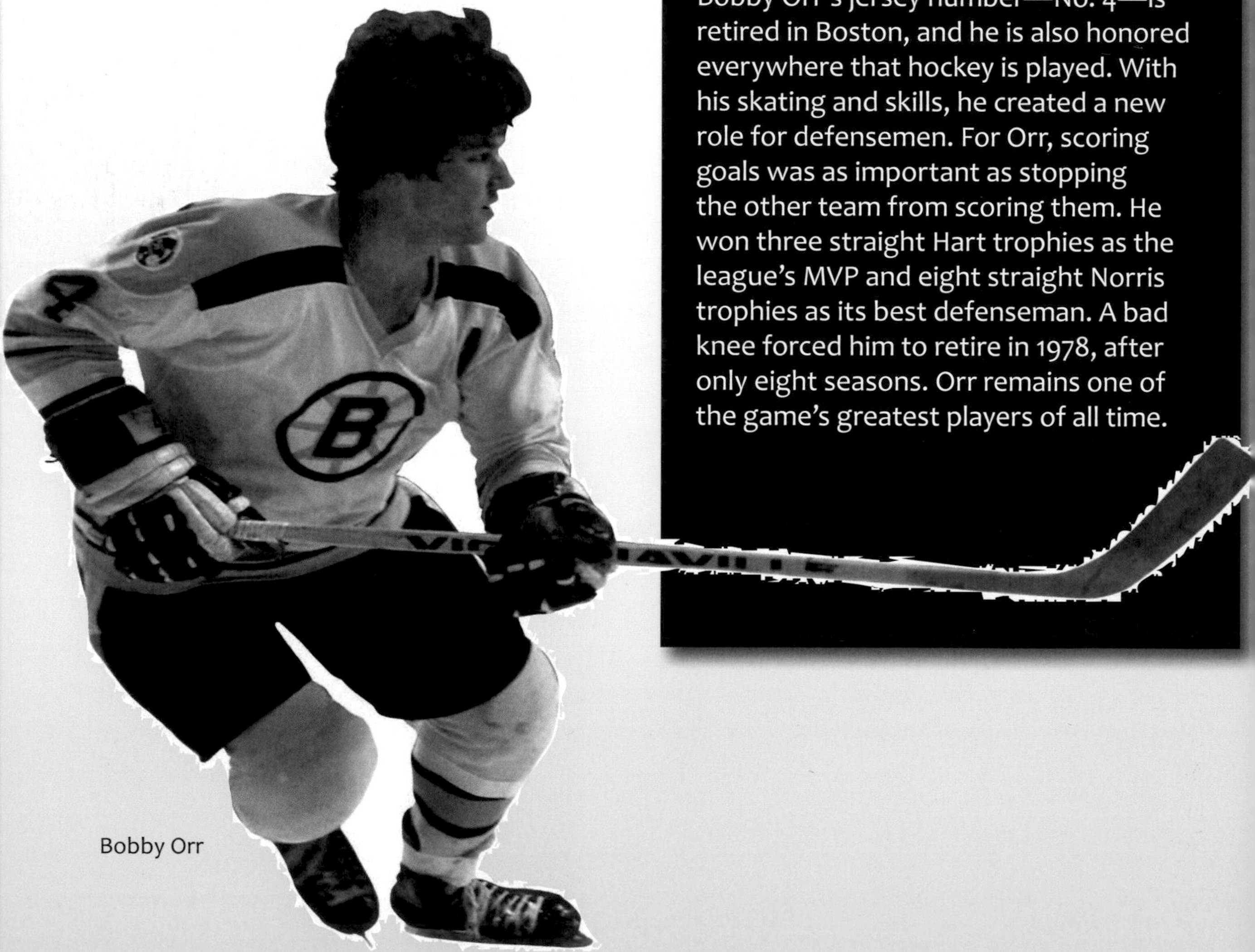

Bobby Orr

Bobby Orr is tripped after he scores the winning goal against the St. Louis Blues.

St. Louis played very tough in Game 4, with a rough defense and hard-hitting body checks to the Bruins players. It was Boston, however, that scored first. St. Louis came back and scored two quick goals to take a 2–1 lead. Boston's regular season star, Esposito, tied the game at 2–2. The Blues' Larry Keenan scored early in the last period to give the Blues a slim 3–2 lead. With six minutes left, Boston scored again, tying the game at 3–3. The game was forced into overtime.

Orr's greatest moment came in overtime. He flipped the puck into the goal for the game winner. Right after he scored, Orr was tripped up by Noel Picard. He went flying arms first through the air, completely level with the ice. The photo of that moment is one of the most famous hockey images of all time. The Stanley Cup victory was one of the great moments in the history of the city of Boston, which had waited 29 years to win the Cup again. Fans would have to wait only two years for the next, with Orr again scoring the series-winning goals.

First Season: 1970–1971

Franchise Record: 1,611–1,291–409–99

Home Rink: First Niagara Center (18,690 capacity) in Buffalo, New York

STANLEY CUPS

None

When the NHL expanded for the first time after doubling the league in 1967, it added a team in Buffalo, New York. Buffalo had a successful minor-league hockey team for 30 years. The Sabres continued that success, reaching two Stanley Cup finals. However, they fell short of a championship each time, despite stars Gilbert Perreault and Dominik Hasek leading the way.

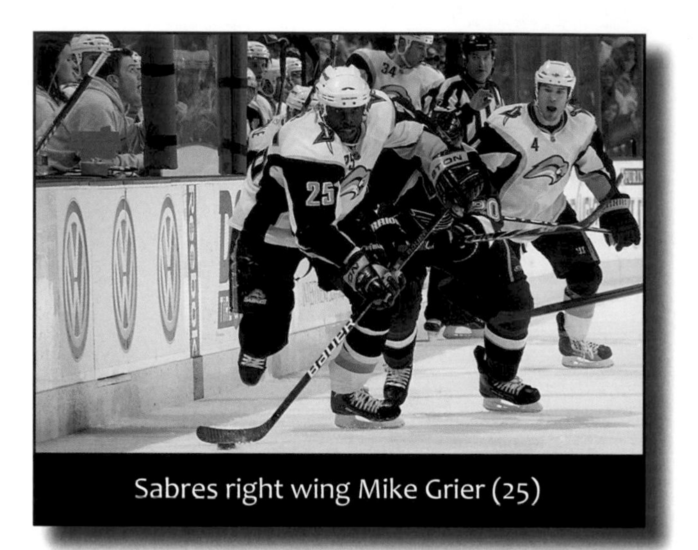

Sabres right wing Mike Grier (25)

Dominik Hasek (39)

Dominik Hasek	G	1992–2001	Won both of his Hart trophies and six Vezina trophies while playing for Buffalo
Pat LaFontaine	C	1991–1997	Retired as the second-highest-scoring American-born player with 1,013 points
Rick Martin	LW	1971–1981	Selected to seven All-Star Games
Ryan Miller	G	2002–2014	Selected to U.S. Olympic team in 2010
Gilbert Perreault	C	1970–1987	High-scoring forward won the Calder Trophy in 1971

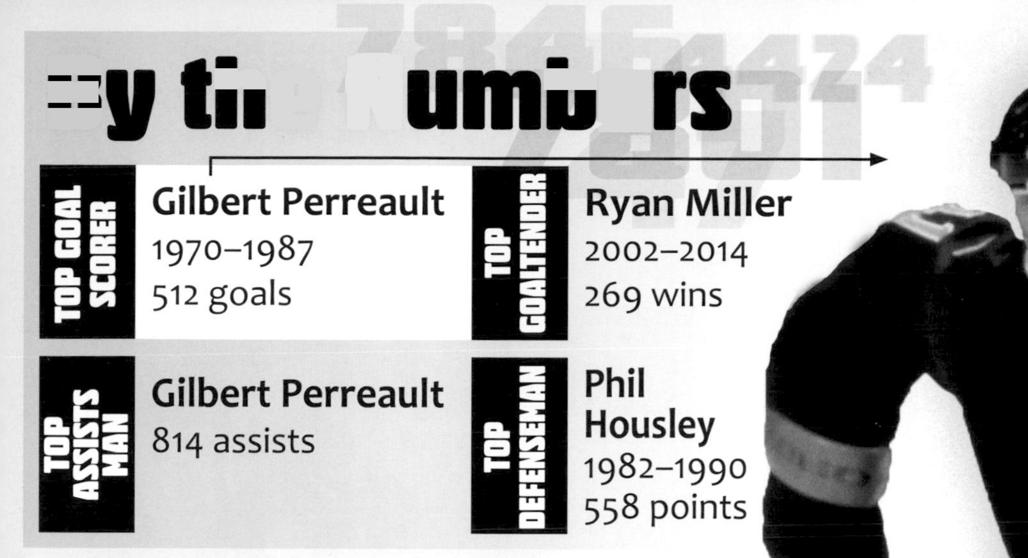

TOP GOAL SCORER	Gilbert Perreault 1970–1987 512 goals	TOP GOALTENDER	Ryan Miller 2002–2014 269 wins
TOP ASSISTS MAN	Gilbert Perreault 814 assists	TOP DEFENSEMAN	Phil Housley 1982–1990 558 points

The French Connection

In the Sabres' early years, the trio of Gilbert Perreault, René Robert, and Rick Martin was a dominating forward line. Since they were all from French-speaking Quebec, the group was dubbed The French Connection. Their nickname was also the name of a popular movie at the time. The line led the Sabres to the 1975 finals, where they lost to the Philadelphia Flyers.

NHL Winter Classic

Outdoor Hockey

The first NHL Winter Classic, an annual New Year's Day outdoor game, took place in Buffalo's Ralph Wilson Stadium in 2008. The Sabres lost to the Pittsburgh Penguins in a shootout that snowy day. It was just the second regular-season outdoor game in NHL history.

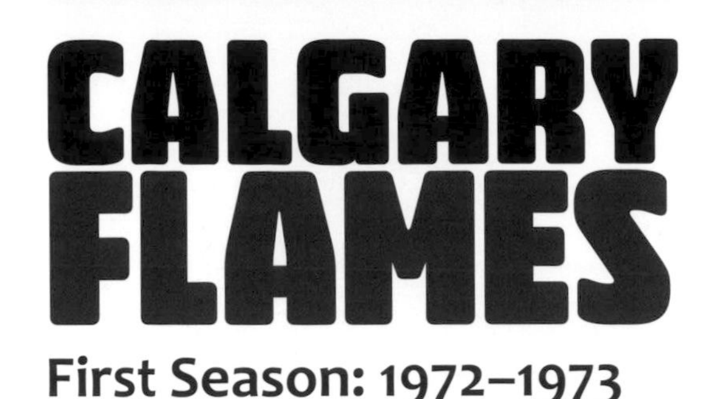

First Season: 1972–1973

Franchise Record: 1,491–1,279–379–105

Home Rink: Scotiabank Saddledome
(19,289 capacity) in Calgary, Alberta, Canada

STANLEY CUP
1989

When the NHL expanded by two teams in 1972, the Canadian province of Alberta wasn't even considered. Instead, Atlanta was the choice, and the Flames were born. But after eight years and limited success, the team packed up and headed north to hockey country. In Calgary the Flames have played for three Stanley Cups, winning the prized trophy once.

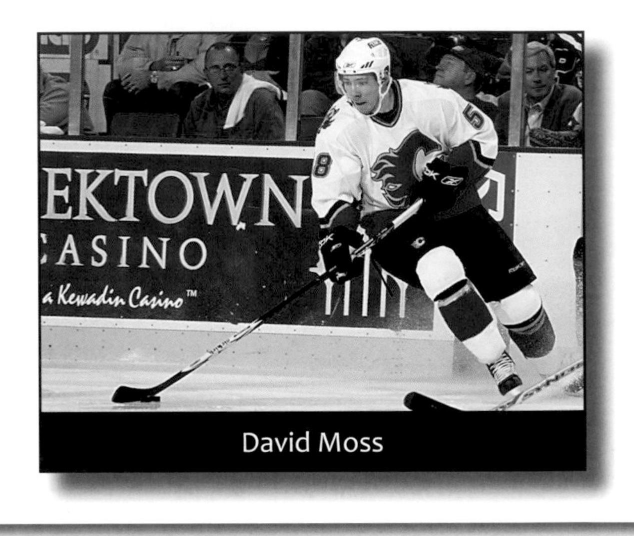

David Moss

Miikka Kiprusoff

Theoren Fleury	RW	1988–1998	Seven-time All-Star Game participant
Jarome Iginla	RW	1996–2013	Six-time All-Star led the NHL in scoring twice
Miikka Kiprusoff	G	2003–2013	Awarded the Vezina Trophy in 2006
Al MacInnis	D	1981–1994	Won the Conn Smythe Trophy in 1989

By the Numbers

TOP GOAL SCORER	**Jarome Iginla** 1996–2013 525 goals
TOP GOALTENDER	**Miikka Kiprusoff** 2003–2013 305 wins
TOP ASSISTS MAN	**Al MacInnis** 1981–1994 609 assists
TOP DEFENSEMAN	**Al MacInnis** 822 points

Rare Win

The Flames captured the 1989 Stanley Cup by winning Game 6 of the finals. That game took place in Montreal, home of the mighty Canadiens. The win was significant because Flames veteran Lanny McDonald and his teammates became the first visiting team to celebrate a championship in the Canadiens' rink.

Calgary coach Darryl Sutter led the Flames to two playoff appearances.

All in the Family

The Sutter boys from tiny Viking, Alberta, are a hockey success story. Six brothers—Brent, Brian, Darryl, Duane, Rich, and Ron—all made it to the NHL. The Sutters have a close connection with the Flames. Ron played for the team, and Brent, Brian, and Darryl all coached it. Darryl led Calgary to the Cup finals in 2004. Two of the brothers' sons also played in the NHL. Darryl's son Brett debuted with the Flames in 2008–2009.

CAROLINA HURRICANES

First Season: 1979–1980

Franchise Record: 1,104–1,230–263–101

Home Rink: PNC Arena (18,730 capacity) in Raleigh, North Carolina

STANLEY CUP
2006

The Carolina Hurricanes' history goes back to another city and another league. They started as the New England Whalers of the World Hockey Association (WHA) in 1972 and were one of four WHA teams to merge into the NHL in 1979 (see page 24). After spending 18 more seasons in Hartford, Connecticut, the team moved to Raleigh, North Carolina, in 1997 and became the Hurricanes.

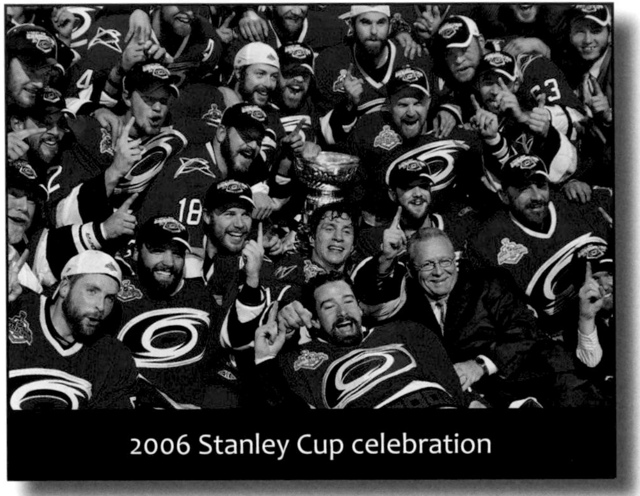

2006 Stanley Cup celebration

Legends & Stars

Cam Ward

Rod Brind'Amour	C	2000–2010	Twice named the NHL's top defensive forward
Ron Francis	C	1981–1991, 1998–2004	Ranks second all-time in assists, third all-time in games played
Eric Staal	C	2003–present	Four-time All-Star Game pick
Cam Ward	G	2005–present	Won the Conn Smythe Trophy in 2006

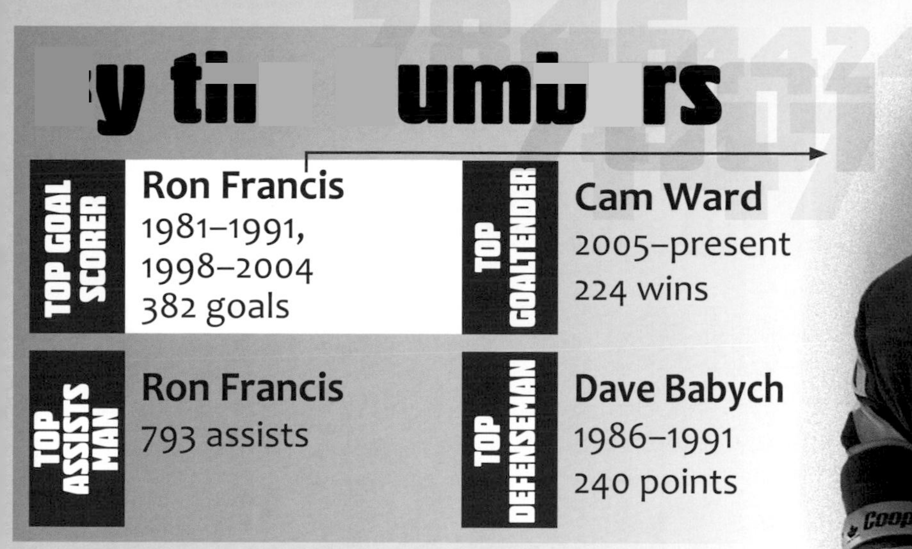

And Howe (and Howe and Howe)

In 1977 the Whalers lured hockey legend Gordie Howe and his sons, defensemen Mark and Marty, to play for the team. They skated together for three seasons, including one year in the NHL when Gordie Howe was 51 years old. The longtime Red Wings star scored 15 goals and had 26 assists in his 32nd and final full year of professional hockey.

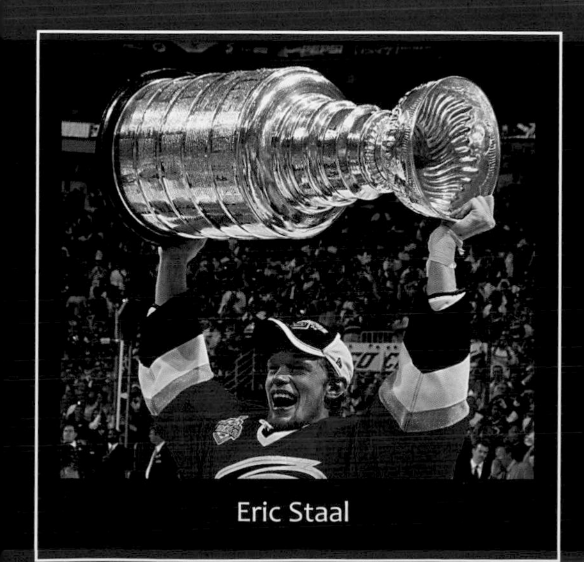

Eric Staal

Carolina Cup

The Hurricanes made it to the Stanley Cup finals in 2002, but they fell to the mighty Red Wings. Four years later, though, high-scoring center Eric Staal was skating the famous trophy around the rink after defeating the Edmonton Oilers. It was the state of North Carolina's first professional sports championship.

CHICAGO BLACKHAWKS

Franchise Record: 2,542–2,556–814–112

Home Rink: United Center (19,717 capacity) in Chicago, Illinois

STANLEY CUPS

1934, 1938, 1961, 2010, 2013

First Season: 1926–1927

One of the NHL's "Original Six" teams, the Chicago Blackhawks were founded by coffee tycoon Major Frederic McLaughlin. To fill up his first roster, McLaughlin purchased Oregon's Portland Rosebuds of the Western Hockey League. Then he moved most of the players to the Windy City.

Commissioner Gary Bettman hands the 2013 Stanley Cup to Jonathan Toews (19).

Patrick Kane

Player	Pos.	Years	Notes
Chris Chelios	D	1990–1999	Won two of his three Norris trophies as a Blackhawk
Tony Esposito	G	1969–1984	Three-time Vezina Trophy winner and six-time All-Star
Glenn Hall	G	1957–1967	Three-time Vezina Trophy winner appeared in 502 consecutive games
Bobby Hull	LW	1957–1972	Won two Hart trophies and played in 12 All-Star Games
Patrick Kane	RW	2007–present	Won the Calder Trophy in 2008
Stan Mikita	C/RW	1958–1980	Two-time Hart and Lady Byng trophy winner
Pierre Pilote	D	1955–1968	Won the Norris Trophy three times in a row
Denis Savard	C	1980–1990, 1995–1997	Seven-time All-Star Game selection
Jonathan Toews	C	2007–present	All-Rookie pick was named captain in his second season

Unlikely Championship

In 1938 the Blackhawks went 14–25–9 but managed to slip into the playoffs. Led by American goaltender Mike Karakas, Chicago upset the Montreal Canadiens and the New York Americans. Then they defeated the Toronto Maple Leafs in the Stanley Cup finals three games to one for their second championship.

Bobby Hull

The Golden Jet

In the late 1950s, a speedy, blond-haired left wing burst onto the ice for the Blackhawks. Bobby Hull, nicknamed "The Golden Jet" because of his yellow locks, could fire a slap shot up to 120 miles (193 kilometers) per hour. To make matters worse for goaltenders, he was one of the first players to add a curve to the blade of his stick, which made the puck fly unpredictably.

COLORADO AVALANCHE

First Season: 1979–1980

Franchise Record: 1,242–1,108–261–87

Home Rink: Pepsi Center
(18,007 capacity) in Denver, Colorado

STANLEY CUPS
1996, 2001

The NHL didn't last long its first time in Denver. In 1982 after just six years, the Colorado Rockies became the New Jersey Devils. But in 1995 another struggling franchise was on the move. The Quebec Nordiques, a World Hockey Association team that had merged into the NHL, moved west and became the Colorado Avalanche.

Patrick Roy blocks a shot during the 2001 playoffs.

Peter Forsberg

Peter Forsberg	C	1994–2004, 2007–2008	Owns a Calder and a Hart trophy
Milan Hejduk	RW	1998–present	Led the NHL in goals in 2002–2003
Patrick Roy	G	1995–2003	Three-time Vezina Trophy winner ranks No. 2 on all-time wins list
Joe Sakic	C	1988–2009	1996 Conn Smythe winner and 2001 Hart Trophy winner
Paul Stastny	C	2006–2014	Named to U.S. Olympic Team in 2010
Peter Stastny	C	1980–1990	Was the Nordiques' all-time leading scorer; still ranks second on the franchise list

TOP GOAL SCORER	Joe Sakic 1988–2009 625 goals	TOP GOALTENDER	Patrick Roy 1995–2003 262 wins
TOP ASSISTS MAN	Joe Sakic 1,016 assists	TOP DEFENSEMAN	Adam Foote 1991–2004, 2008–2011 259 points

Stastny Scores

In the early 1980s, three brothers from the country formerly known as Czechoslovakia—Peter, Anton, and Marian Stastny—went to Canada and played for the Quebec Nordiques. Peter became one of the top scorers not named Gretzky to skate in the NHL. The Nordiques retired Stastny's No. 26 jersey, but his son, Paul wore it for the Avs for eight seasons when he was with the team.

Paul Stastny

Ready to Win

In their last season in Quebec City, the Nordiques lost in the first round of the post-season. But with players such as Joe Sakic, Peter Forsberg, Valeri Kamensky, and Claude Lemieux, the franchise was ready for greatness. The next season the team had transformed into the Avalanche, traded for Hall-of-Fame goaltender Patrick Roy, and won the Stanley Cup.

2000-2001 COLORADO AVALANCHE

After moving to Denver from Quebec City in 1995, the Avalanche quickly became one of the NHL's most successful franchises. Joe Sakic and Peter Forsberg, two of the game's best forwards, were already on board as well as the game's best goalie, Patrick Roy. They won their first Stanley Cup in 1996.

The Avalanche score against the New Jersey Devils in Game 1 of the Stanley Cup finals.

For the team's 2000–2001 season, they were joined by a new star. Ray Bourque was one of the best defensemen of his generation. He had spent all 20 seasons of his career in Boston. After two unsuccessful trips to the finals with the Bruins, Bourque wanted another chance to win the Cup before his career ended. He asked for a trade to Colorado in 2000.

That year, the Avalanche had the best regular season record, 52–16–10–4 (Wins–Losses–Ties–Overtime Losses). Roy made history as he broke Terry Sawchuck's record for career wins, with 448. After avoiding Detroit and Dallas in the playoffs, the Avalanche would face the Devils in the finals. Bourque and Colorado could not be stopped.

2000–2001 Record

Won	Lost	Tied	OTL	Playoffs
52	16	10	4	Defeated Vancouver Canucks 4–0
				Defeated Los Angeles Kings 4–3
				Defeated St. Louis Blues 4–1
				Defeated New Jersey Devils 4–3

Bourque's motto was "16W"—the number of wins needed to win the Cup, and the exit off the New Jersey Turnpike that led to the Meadowlands, where the Devils played.

In Game 1, the Avalanche came out strong behind two goals from star Sakic and one each from Rob Blake, Chris Drury, and Steven Reinprecht. The Avalanche won easily, 5–0, shutting out the Devils. Roy was great in the win, stopping all 26 shots he faced. It was his third playoff shutout, and eighteenth of the year, as he extended his Stanley Cup winning streak to nine games.

New Jersey came back in Game 2. Colorado's Sakic scored the first goal of the game with only six minutes played, but his team would not score again. The Devils came back in the first period. Neither of the teams scored again, but that was enough to lead New Jersey to a 2–1 victory, as they tied the series up at 1–1.

The Avalanche started out Game 3 losing 1–0, but Martin Skoula, Bourque, and Dan Hinote all scored goals, giving their team a 3–1 victory and a 2–1 series lead. However, New Jersey wasn't about to lose two games in a row. They outshot the Avalanche 35–12 in Game 4 and ended up with a 3–2 victory. The series was tied 2–2.

HISTORY BOX

THE DEAD PUCK ERA

The Colorado Avalanche were one of the few teams in the league with plenty of offensive talent. At this time, most teams were concentrating on defense and making it almost impossible for other teams to score. When the Devils won the Cup in 1995, they did it with a system known as the "neutral-zone trap," which puts lots of players in the middle of the ice and reduces offensive chances. By 2000 nearly every team in the league was using a method of the trap. In 1983–1984 the Oilers scored 446 goals. In 2002–2003 no team scored more than 269, and two teams scored fewer than two goals per game.

Patrick Roy

Patrick Roy retired in 2003 with a claim to the title of hockey's greatest goaltender ever. He won the Stanley Cup with Montreal as a rookie in 1986, and he then led the Canadiens to glory in 1993. But in December 1995, Montreal coach Mario Tremblay refused to take him out of the net on a night when the Canadiens lost 11–1. When he was finally replaced, Roy said he would never play for Montreal again. Traded to Colorado, he led the Avalanche to the Stanley Cup that season and another in 2001. He is the NHL's all-time leader in games played by a goalie (1,029), wins (551), and playoff wins (151).

Patrick Roy

Game 5 went to New Jersey, who won 4–1. This loss was Colorado's worst loss of the post-season. Until this game, they had not trailed in the playoffs by more than one goal. It was also the first time they lost back-to-back playoff games. Instead of feeling sorry for themselves, they came out strong in Game 6. Roy recorded his second shutout of the series, and fourth of the playoffs, as Colorado won 4–0. Roy blocked all 24 shots that came at him, including 12 in the first period. Adam Foote, Ville Nieminen, Drury, and Alex Tanguay all scored goals for the Avalanche, tying the series at 3–3. This forced a seventh game at their home arena.

No one in the history of the NHL waited as long as Bourque to win the Stanley Cup, and he finally got it in Game 7. Sakic scored a goal and assisted on one in the game, bringing his total to 13 goals and 13 assists for the playoffs. Tanguay was the star of the game, scoring two goals to lead the Avalanche to a 3–1 victory, and their second Stanley Cup in five years. Roy had 25 stops, and because of his excellent play in the playoffs, he was awarded the Conn Smythe Trophy.

After the victory, NHL Commissioner Gary Bettman handed the Cup to Avalanche captain Sakic to hoist above his head. But instead of lifting the Cup, Sakic passed it to Bourque. After 22 seasons in the NHL, Bourque capped his Hall of Fame career by raising the Cup above his head.

A promising team became a great one after Ray Bourque joined.

COLUMBUS BLUE JACKETS

Franchise Record: 409–490–33–100

Home Rink: Nationwide Arena (18,136 capacity) in Columbus, Ohio

STANLEY CUPS

NONE

First Season: 2000–2001

The second go-round of NHL hockey in Ohio has been more successful than the first. In 1976 the California Golden Seals moved to Cleveland and became known as the Barons. But that team lasted just two seasons before folding. More than 20 years later, Ohio's capital, Columbus, was awarded an expansion team, and the Blue Jackets were born.

Raffi Torres (14) controls the puck near the Red Wings' net during the 2009 playoffs.

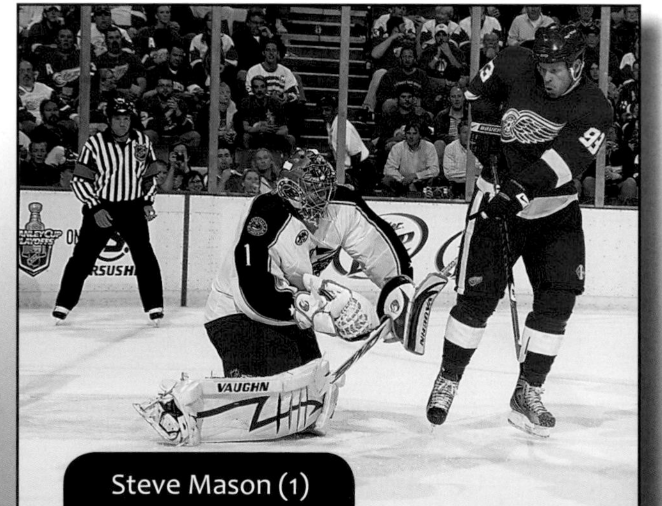

Steve Mason (1)

Sergei Bobrovsky	G	2012–present	Won the Vezina Trophy in 2013
Rostislav Klesla	D	2000–2011	Selected to the NHL All-Rookie Team in 2001–2002
Steve Mason	G	2008–2013	Calder Trophy winner and Vezina runner-up in 2009
Rick Nash	LW	2002–2012	Five-time All-Star led the league in goals in 2004
R. J. Umberger	C	2008-present	Ranks third in franchise history in points

Rick Nash
2002–2012
289 goals

Rick Nash
258 assists

Steve Mason
2008–2013
96 wins

Fedor Tyutin
2008–present
141 points →

Young Gun

Columbus made the right call picking Rick Nash with the No. 1 overall draft pick in 2002. By the end of the 2003–2004 season, the 19-year-old Nash was the youngest player in NHL history to lead the league in goals. He was also an All-Star that season, becoming the youngest to play in the game since 1986.

Rick Nash (61) won the Maurice Richard Trophy in 2003–2004.

Tragedy at the Rink

In 2002 Brittanie Cecil, a 13-year-old fan, was struck by a puck that had deflected into the stands at Nationwide Arena. She died two days later from the injury. She was the first fan to die in the 85-year history of the NHL. As a result the teams decided to hang netting behind the goals at all arenas to prevent such a tragedy from happening again.

First Season: 1967–1968

Franchise Record: 1,572–1,510–459–95

Home Rink: American Airlines Center (18,000 capacity) in Dallas, Texas

STANLEY CUP

1999

For 26 seasons the North Stars played in the Twin Cities of Minneapolis and St. Paul. But in 1993 the team moved to Texas, dropped the word North from its name, and became the Dallas Stars. In Minnesota the Stars went to two Stanley Cup finals, but they finally won a title in Dallas in 1999.

Brett Hull (22) takes a shot against the Colorado Avalanche during the 1999 playoffs.

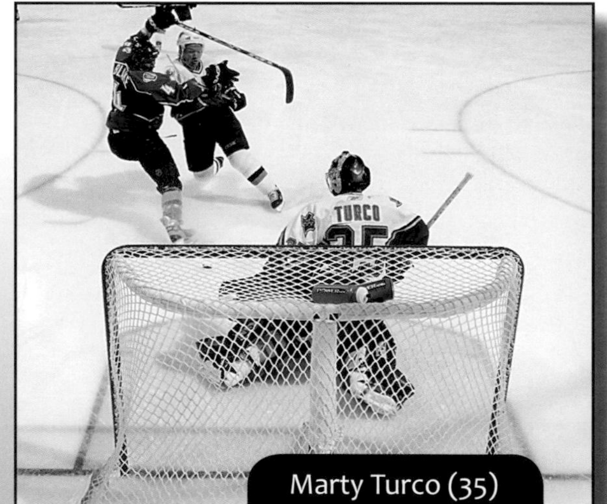

Marty Turco (35)

Ed Belfour	G	1997–2002	Allowed the fewest goals in the NHL four times
Neal Broten	C	1980–1995, 1996–1997	Team's all-time leading scorer during the Minnesota years
Loui Eriksson	LW	2006–2013	Left wing became an All-Star in 2011
Mike Modano	C	1989–2010	Named to seven All-Star Games in 20 years with the Stars
Joe Nieuwendyk	C	1995–2002	Conn Smythe Trophy winner in 1999
Marty Turco	G	2000–2010	Three-time All-Star Game selection

TOP GOAL SCORER
Mike Modano
1989–2010
557 goals

TOP GOALTENDER
Marty Turco
2000–2010
262 wins

TOP ASSISTS MAN
Mike Modano
802 assists

TOP DEFENSEMAN
Sergei Zubov
1996–2009
549 points

Epic Win

When Brett Hull scored the Stanley Cup-clinching goal in the third overtime of Game 6 in the 1999 finals, it was the end of a marathon night. The Stars and the Sabres battled for 114 minutes, 51 seconds and combined for 104 shots on goal. Dallas goalie Ed Belfour made 53 saves in the 2-1 Stars victory.

Stars right wing Pat Verbeek (16) fights for the puck during the 1999 Stanley Cup finals.

American Hero

The Minnesota North Stars drafted Mike Modano with the No. 1 overall pick in 1988. He played 20 of his 21 seasons with the Stars. As well as being the franchise's all-time leading scorer, he was also the NHL's top scoring American-born player. He finished his career with 1,374 points.

DETROIT RED WINGS

First Season: 1926–1927

Franchise Record: 2,774–2,328–815–107

Home Rink: Joe Louis Arena (20,066 capacity) in Detroit, Michigan

STANLEY CUPS

1936, 1937, 1943, 1950, 1952, 1954, 1955, 1997, 1998, 2002, 2008

With 11 NHL championships—more than any other hockey team in the United States—Detroit earned the nickname "Hockeytown." Only the Canadiens and the Maple Leafs have more Stanley Cup wins. First known as the Detroit Cougars and then the Falcons, the team became the Red Wings in 1932.

Nicklas Lidstrom hoists the Stanley Cup after the 2008 Finals.

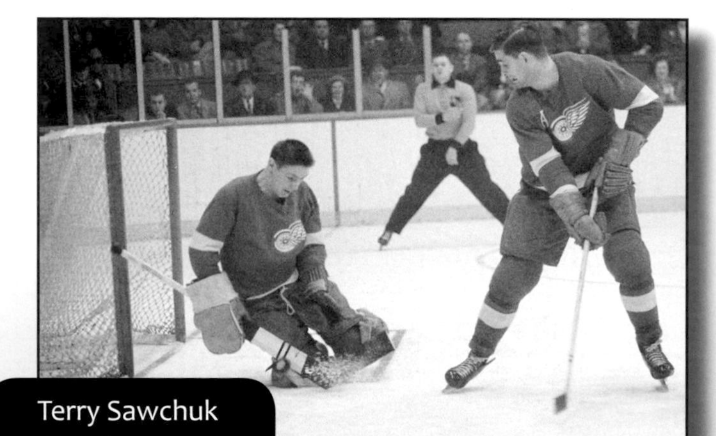

Terry Sawchuk

Jack Adams		1927–1947	Wings' second coach won three championships in 20 years
Alex Delvecchio	C/LW	1950–1974	Named to the All-Star Game 13 times in 24 seasons
Sergei Fedorov	C	1990–2003	Won the Hart Trophy once and the Frank J. Selke Trophy twice
Gordie Howe	RW	1946–1971	Six-time Hart Trophy winner ranks third on the all-time points list
Red Kelly	D	1947–1960	Captured four Lady Byng awards and one Norris Trophy
Nicklas Lidstrom	D	1991–2012	Owns seven Norris trophies and one Conn Smythe Trophy
Ted Lindsay	LW	1944–1957, 1964–1965	Captained three Stanley Cup winners in the 1950s
Chris Osgood	G	1993–2001, 2005–2011	Two-time Jennings Trophy winner
Terry Sawchuk	G	1949–1955, 1957–1964, 1968–1969	Four-time Vezina Trophy winner
Steve Yzerman	C	1983–2006	1998 Conn Smythe winner played 22 seasons in Detroit

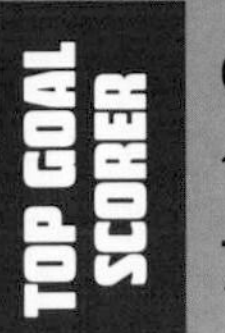

y th umb rs

TOP GOAL SCORER	**Gordie Howe** 1946–1971 786 goals	TOP GOALTENDER	**Terry Sawchuk** 1949–1955, 1957–1964, 1968–1969 351 wins
TOP ASSISTS MAN	**Steve Yzerman** 1983–2006 1,063 assists	TOP DEFENSEMAN	**Nicklas Lidstrom** 1991–2012 1,142 points

Mr. Hockey

There's a reason Gordie Howe got the nickname "Mr. Hockey": He could do it all. In more than 25 seasons in Detroit, Howe led the league in scoring six times. In 14 other seasons, he ranked among the top five, and he finished his NHL career with 1,850 points and four championships. (For more on Howe, turn to page 52.)

Throwing the Octopus

A slimy tradition started in 1952. That's when a dead octopus was first thrown onto the ice during a Red Wings home playoff game for good luck. The creature's eight legs then represented the eight wins a team needed to win the Stanley Cup. Even though more games are now needed, the smelly tradition continues.

1954-1955 DETROIT RED WINGS

Detroit Red Wings star Gordie Howe played hockey throughout five decades and enjoyed individual success throughout his years as a player. Howe won four Stanley Cups with the Red Wings in the early 1950s. The Detroit Red Wings finished first in the league seven straight times from 1948–1949 through 1954–1955.

Gordie Howe (1928-)

Gordie Howe was among the NHL's top-five scorers for 20 straight seasons. He led the league in scoring six times and was named MVP six times. In the process Howe set records for games played, points, goals, and assists.

It wasn't until Wayne Gretzky came along that Howe's records were broken. The two played together in the World Hockey Association (WHA). In 1979–1980, when that league merged with the NHL, Gretzky's first NHL season was Howe's last. In 1997 Howe actually played with the minor-league Detroit Vipers to reach the milestone of five decades of playing pro hockey.

In addition to Howe, the Red Wings were a great team. In 1954–1955, the Red Wings had the best offensive attack in hockey, with the high-scoring, hard-hitting "Production Line" of Howe, "Terrible" Ted Lindsay, and Alex Delvecchio. In 1952–1953, Howe led the league with 95 points, and Lindsay was second with 71, as the Red Wings scored 222 goals. None of the other five teams in the NHL scored more than 169 goals.

Terry Sawchuk

HISTORY BOX

THE MOTOR CITY WORK ETHIC

"The Production Line" was a good nickname for the Red Wings' top forward line of Gordie Howe, Ted Lindsay, and Alex Delvecchio. Not only could that line score lots of goals, the players also represented the spirit of the city. In the years after World War II (1939–1945), there was a huge growth of the auto industry in Detroit, Michigan. Many fans worked on the production line in an auto plant, such as Ford's massive River Rouge complex, and then relaxed by watching the Red Wings play. In a hardworking city, the Red Wings were especially appreciated because they tried hard in every game.

After their seventh straight first-place finish, the Red Wings faced the Toronto Maple Leafs in the first round of the playoffs. They easily beat Toronto in four games, moving on to the Stanley Cup finals, where they faced the Montreal Canadiens. The Canadiens had reached the finals for their fifth straight year. The two teams had met earlier in the regular season, when both teams were tied for first place. Montreal's fans had gotten out of control and started a riot.

Inside the arena, the fans threw food, programs, and a tear gas bomb. Outside, they ran wild in the street, smashing windows and breaking into stores and cars. Because of the riot, tensions between the teams and their fans were very high. It would be an interesting matchup.

In Game 1 of the Stanley Cup finals, Detroit's Marty Pavelich and Lindsay scored goals late in the game to lead the Red Wings to a 4–2 victory. Lindsay continued his great playing in Game 2, scoring an amazing four goals to lead the Red Wings to an easy 7–1 victory. Marcel Pronovost, Howe, and Delvecchio also scored for Detroit. Detroit now led the

Ted Lindsay scored many goals for the Red Wings.

1954-1955 Record

Won	Lost	Tied	Playoffs
42	17	11	Defeated Toronto Maple Leafs 4–0
			Defeated Montreal Canadiens 4–3

series, 2–0. However, Montreal didn't give up. They came back in Game 3 and won behind Bernie "Boom-Boom" Geoffrion's two goals. Montreal then used the momentum from their Game 3 win and won Game 4 against Detroit, 5–3. Earl "Dutch" Reibel tried to keep the Red Wings in the game by scoring two goals, but it just wasn't enough.

The series was now tied 2–2. Playing great like he had been all season, Howe scored a hat trick for his team, and they cruised to a 5–1 victory in Game 5. All Detroit needed was one more victory to win the Stanley Cup, but Montreal wasn't ready to give up. In Game 6 the Canadiens showed they wanted to be champions just as much as the Red Wings did. They won 6–3. The series was now tied 3–3, and the final Game 7 would determine which team would be crowned champion. People started to call the series a "homer's series," because every victory in the series was won at the home team's arena.

Game 7 was intense. It was at the Red Wings' arena, and the team hadn't lost a home game in four months. The "Production Line" carried them through. They weren't going to let the Canadiens beat them at home, and they won an exciting 3–1 game to clinch the Stanley Cup. Delvecchio was the offensive star of the game, scoring two goals, while Howe added one, his ninth goal of the playoffs. Howe set a playoff record with 20 points in 11 games. The victory gave Detroit's general manager, Jack Adams, his seventh Stanley Cup!

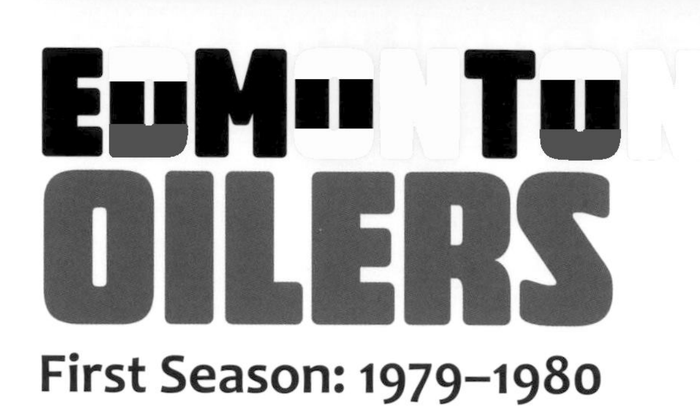

First Season: 1979–1980

Franchise Record: 1,224–1,102–262–110

Home Rink: Rexall Place (16,839 capacity) in Edmonton, Alberta, Canada

STANLEY CUPS

1984, 1985, 1987, 1988, 1990

One of four World Hockey Association (WHA) teams to join the NHL, the Edmonton Oilers became a dynasty in the 1980s, thanks to "The Great One"—Wayne Gretzky. The superstar and his high-flying, high-scoring supporting cast scored 400 goals a season five years in a row. That run included an NHL-record 446 goals over 80 games (5.6 per game) during the Alberta team's first Stanley Cup season in 1983–1984. (For more on this amazing season, turn the page.)

Coach Craig MacTavish won more than 300 games in eight seasons with the Oilers.

Taylor Hall

Glenn Anderson	RW	1980–1991, 1996	Four-time All-Star Game selection
Paul Coffey	D	1980–1987	Three-time Norris Trophy winner and a 14-time All-Star Game pick
Grant Fuhr	G	1981–1991	Won the Vezina Trophy in 1988
Wayne Gretzky	C	1978–1988	NHL's all-time leading scorer won nine Hart trophies in 10 years
Taylor Hall	LW	2010–present	NHL's top overall pick in 2010
Jari Kurri	RW	1980–1990	Ranks second on the Oilers' all-time scoring list
Mark Messier	C	1979–1991	Two-time MVP ranks second on the NHL's all-time points list
Glen Sather		1976–1989, 1993–1994	Edmonton coach led the Oilers to four Stanley Cup championships

By the Numbers

TOP GOAL SCORER	Wayne Gretzky 1978–1988 583 goals	TOP GOALTENDER	Grant Fuhr 1981–1991 226 wins
TOP ASSISTS MAN	Wayne Gretzky 1,086 assists	TOP DEFENSEMAN	Paul Coffey 1980–1987 669 points

How Great?

It's safe to say that Wayne Gretzky's records will never be broken. Number 99 was the only player to score more than 200 points in a season. He accomplished the feat four times, including a record 215-point performance (52 goals, 163 assists) in 1985–1986. Gretzky scored a record 92 goals in 1981–1982. His career-points mark of 2,857 includes 1,963 assists, which is more than the total points compiled by anyone else who's ever played.

Mess and the Rest

If people needed proof that the Oilers were more than just Wayne Gretzky, they got it in 1990. Two years after Gretzky was traded to the Kings (see page 59), Edmonton won another Stanley Cup. That team included captain Mark Messier and six others who were part of all five of the Oilers' championships.

1983-1984 EDMONTON OILERS

The greatest player the game of hockey has ever known, Wayne Gretzky, could do anything. He set records for goals, assists, and points in a career and in a single season that may never be broken. He retired with 61 NHL records. He played on many great teams, but the 1983–1984 Edmonton Oilers were the best.

To win his first Stanley Cup, Gretzky had to beat the New York Islanders in 1984. The Islanders had won four Stanley Cups in a row, and in 1982–1983, the Islanders had beaten the Oilers for the Cup. The Oilers' coach, Glen Sather, had promised that the next season his team would score 100 points, win the division, and win the Stanley Cup. Sather stuck to his word, as the 1983–1984 Oilers achieved every goal he set for them. Edmonton won the Cup and became hockey's new dynasty. The Oilers would win four Cups in five years.

With Gretzky in the middle, the Oilers were the best offensive team ever. The 1983–1984 Oilers won 57 games and set a record with 446 goals. Gretzky, Jari Kurri, and Glenn Anderson all scored 50 or more goals for the Oilers. Only the great Mario Lemieux could keep the

Grant Fuhr (1962-)

Grant Fuhr had a tough job. The Oilers scored so many goals that they didn't have to play much defense. That left him alone as the goalie. His statistics weren't very good, so sometimes fans ignored him. But he was also a pioneer, the game's first great black goalie and one of its first black stars. Ten years after Fuhr played in the NHL, there were more than a dozen African American goalies playing at the top level in hockey. Fuhr was inducted into the Hockey Hall of Fame in 2003.

1983-1984 Record

Won	Lost	Tied	Playoffs
57	18	5	Defeated Winnipeg Jets 3–0
			Defeated Calgary Flames 4–3
			Defeated Minnesota North Stars 4–0
			Defeated New York Islanders 4–1

Oilers from dominating the individual leaders. Twice, the Oilers had three players who were 50-goal scorers and four players who were 100-point scorers. This had never been done before. Grant Fuhr and Mark Messier were also great players.

In the first round of the playoffs, the Oilers faced Winnipeg. The Oilers swept the Jets. In the second round, the Oilers faced a much tougher opponent in the Calgary Flames. The series went all the way to the deciding Game 7, where the Oilers earned the victory to advance to the next round. In the semifinals, the Oilers faced Minnesota, who they easily swept to earn their spot in the Stanley Cup finals.

It was the second straight year they had reached the finals, where they met the New York Islanders, who had beaten them the previous year and were going for their fifth-straight Cup. It would be a great series.

Game 1 of the finals was a great defensive match. No team scored in the first two periods, as Oilers goalie Fuhr and Islanders goalie Billy Smith played incredibly in the net. Someone had to score, and in the third period, Oilers player Kevin McClelland broke free for a goal. It was all Edmonton needed as they shut out the defending champions 1–0.

New York showed why they had won four straight Cups in Game 2 as Clark Gillies scored a hat trick. The Islanders coasted to an easy 6–1 victory, tying the series at 1–1. The teams switched roles in Game 3, as Edmonton did most of the scoring. Edmonton's Glenn Anderson and Paul Coffey scored two goals only 17 seconds apart. They eventually scored five more goals, three coming in the last period, for an easy 7–2 victory. Edmonton now led the series 2–1.

Gretzky scored two goals in Game 4 as the Oilers won again, 7–2. Edmonton led the series 3–1 against the defending champions. With a chance for the Oilers to earn the Stanley Cup if they won in Game 5, Gretzky came out playing great. He scored the first two goals of the game, both on assists by Kurri. Gretzky then showed that he could pass, too, as he assisted Ken Linseman for a goal. Kurri scored one himself and gave the Oilers a strong 4–0 lead. The Islanders tried to come back, but Edmonton was just too strong. The Oilers ended up winning 5–2, clinching the Stanley Cup.

On August 9, 1988, the hockey world was shocked when the Oilers traded Gretzky and two other players to the Kings for two players, three first-round picks, and cash. The Oilers had won four Cups with Gretzky. They won one after he left, but the team was never as good as they were in 1984.

Wayne Gretzky lifts the Stanley Cup in 1984.

HISTORY BOX

GRETZKY GOES WEST

The trade that sent Wayne Gretzky west to the Los Angeles Kings was very surprising. But it changed hockey forever by making it popular in new places. Hockey had always been popular in Canada. Now people in Hollywood liked it, too. The United States was changing. People were moving from states such as Pennsylvania and Ohio to states such as Arizona and California to find work. Soon, the NHL would put teams in those warm-weather places for the fans who moved there. Because of players like Gretzky, people all over the country wanted to be part of the excitement of pro hockey.

First Season: 1993–1994

Franchise Record: 617–677–142–138

Home Rink: BB&T Center (19,250 capacity) in Sunrise, Florida

STANLEY CUPS
None

To say that the Panthers burst onto the NHL scene would be an understatement. The expansion team from south Florida was the most successful first-year team in league history, winning 33 games and compiling 83 points for the Atlantic Division standings in 1993–1994. Two years later the Panthers were competing for the Stanley Cup.

Jay Bouwmeester (4) was selected to the 2007 and 2009 All-Star games.

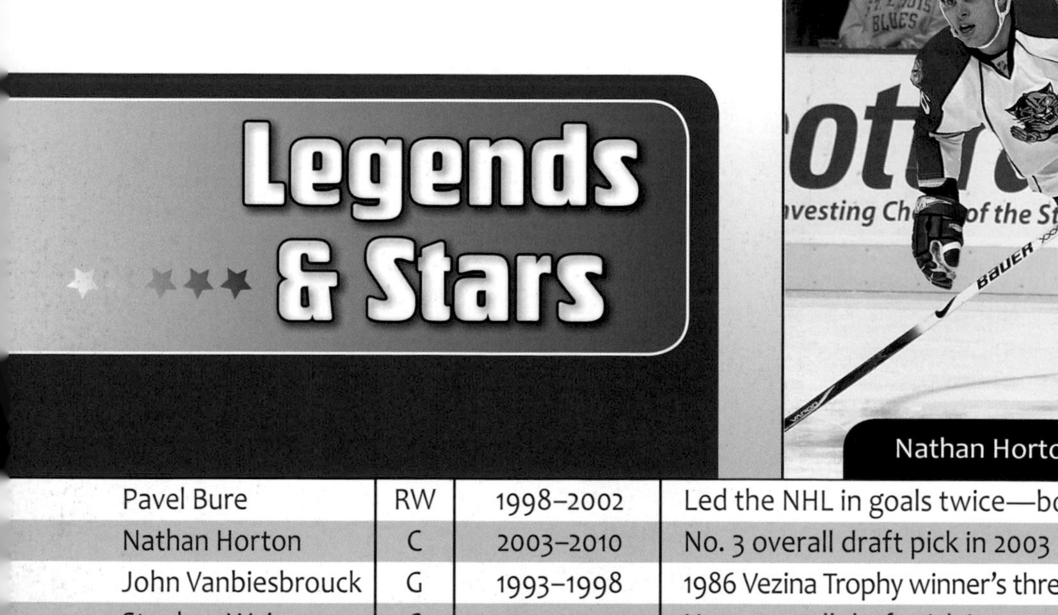

Nathan Horton

Pavel Bure	RW	1998–2002	Led the NHL in goals twice—both times as a Panther
Nathan Horton	C	2003–2010	No. 3 overall draft pick in 2003
John Vanbiesbrouck	G	1993–1998	1986 Vezina Trophy winner's three All-Star seasons were in Florida
Stephen Weiss	C	2001–2013	No. 4 overall draft pick in 2001

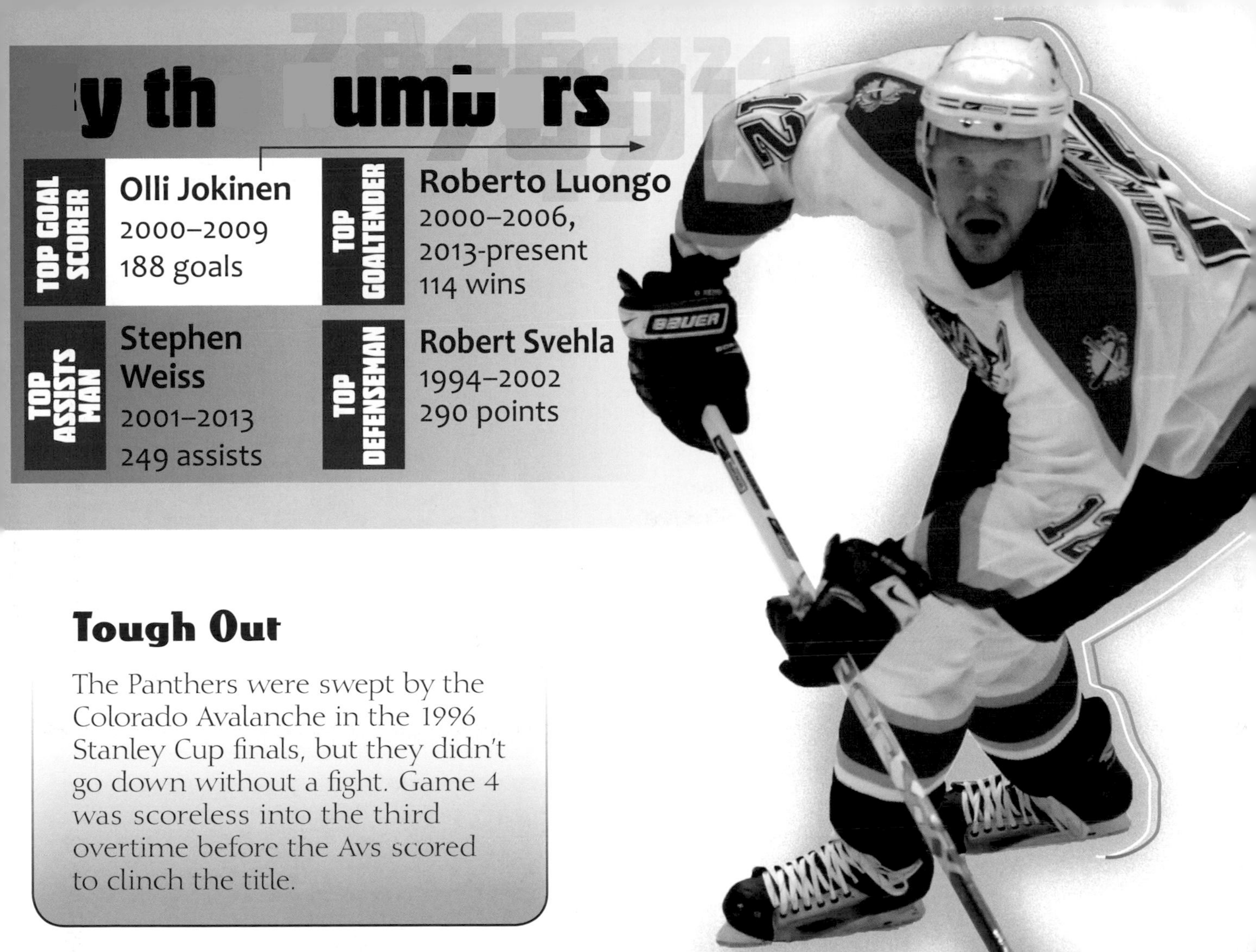

By the Numbers

TOP GOAL SCORER	**Olli Jokinen** 2000–2009 188 goals
TOP GOALTENDER	**Roberto Luongo** 2000–2006, 2013-present 114 wins
TOP ASSISTS MAN	**Stephen Weiss** 2001–2013 249 assists
TOP DEFENSEMAN	**Robert Svehla** 1994–2002 290 points

Tough Out

The Panthers were swept by the Colorado Avalanche in the 1996 Stanley Cup finals, but they didn't go down without a fight. Game 4 was scoreless into the third overtime before the Avs scored to clinch the title.

Rat Trick

On opening night of the 1995-1996 season, a rat scurried across the floor of the Panthers' locker room. Forward Scott Mellanby killed it with a slap shot against the wall. That night Mellanby scored two goals, and goalie John Vanbiesbrouck proclaimed it hockey's first "rat trick." The legend was born. As the season went on, fans threw rubber rats on the ice after Florida's first goal of a game. By the time the Stanley Cup finals came along, more than 2,000 fake rats were thrown onto the ice each game.

LOS ANGELES KINGS

First Season: 1967–1968

Franchise Record: 1,455–1,577–424–98

Home Rink: Staples Center (18,118 capacity) in Los Angeles, California

STANLEY CUP
2012, 2014

The NHL's "Original Six" teams resided in cold-weather cities. But when the league made its first big expansion, it went to sunny southern California, and the Los Angeles Kings were born. The team has boasted electric offensive players, including Marcel Dionne and Wayne Gretzky. As a No. 8 seed in the 2011–2012 playoffs, the Kings won the first of two Stanley Cups.

Kings goalie Jonathan Quick makes a save against the Boston Bruins in 2010.

Legends & Stars

Drew Doughty

Rob Blake	D	1989–2001, 2006–2008	Norris Trophy winner in 1998
Marcel Dionne	C	1975–1987	Ranks fifth on the NHL's all-time scoring list
Drew Doughty	D	2008–present	Second overall draft pick in 2008 and All-Rookie Team pick in 2009
Wayne Gretzky	C	1988–1996	"The Great One" led the NHL in scoring and won one Hart Trophy as a King
Luc Robitaille	LW	1986–2001, 2003–2006	Eight-time All-Star Game pick and Calder Trophy winner
Jonathan Quick	G	2007–present	Won the Conn Smythe Trophy as playoff MVP in 2012

By the Numbers

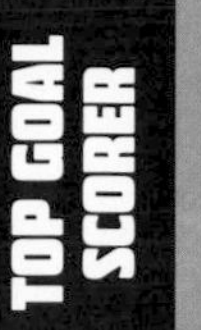

Luc Robitaille
1986–2001,
2003–2006
557 goals

TOP GOALTENDER

Jonathan Quick
2007–present
176 wins

Marcel Dionne
1975–1987
757 assists

Rob Blake →
1989–2001,
2006–2008
494 points

Down but Not Out

Six years before getting "The Great One," the Kings pulled off the unthinkable. They eliminated Gretzky's Oilers from the Stanley Cup playoffs. The series win included a stunning, come-from-behind victory. The Kings were down 5-0 after two periods, but they came back to win 6-5 in overtime.

Trade of the Century

August 9, 1988, is a date that changed the NHL forever. That's when the Edmonton Oilers traded the game's greatest player, Wayne Gretzky, to the Los Angeles Kings. Number 99—now retired by the entire league—played to sellout crowds every night. He led L.A. to its only Stanley Cup finals appearance. After winning four times with the Oilers, however, he couldn't clinch one for the Kings.

Each Kings player wore Gretzky's 99 as a tribute after his number was retired.

MINNESOTA WILD

First Season: 2000–2001

Franchise Record: 474–408–55–95

Home Rink: Xcel Energy Center
(18,064 capacity) in St. Paul, Minnesota

STANLEY CUPS

None

Minnesota is the self-proclaimed "State of Hockey." But after the North Stars left for Dallas in 1993, the state was without an NHL team for seven years. When the league expanded for the last time, it was only natural to go back to a hockey-crazy part of the United States. In 2010 the team played in its 400th home game. Every one of those games was played before a sellout crowd, the third-longest sellout streak in NHL history.

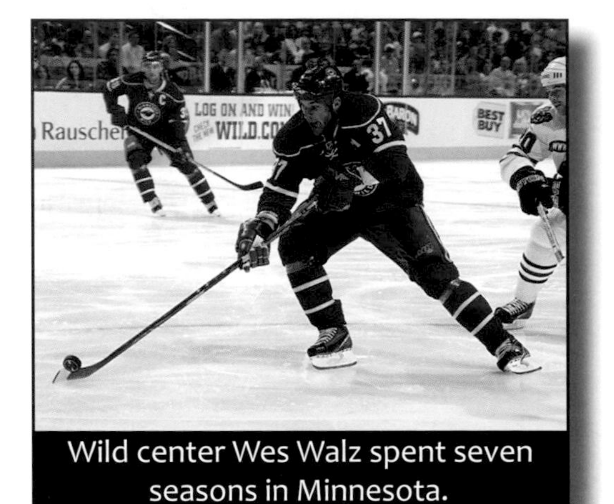

Wild center Wes Walz spent seven seasons in Minnesota.

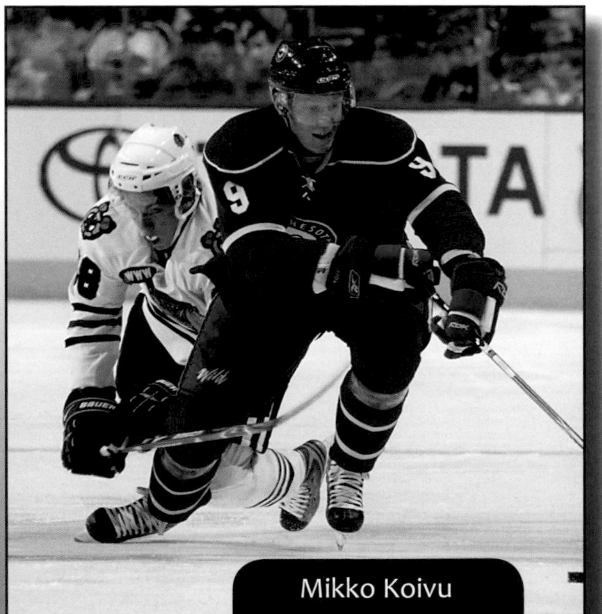
Mikko Koivu

Niklas Backstrom	G	2006–present	Jennings Trophy winner in 2007
Marian Gaborik	RW	2000–2009	Two-time All-Star Game selection
Mikko Koivu	C	2005–present	Wild captain was a first-round draft pick in 2001
Zach Parise	LW	2012–present	Led Wild in goals and points during first season
Ryan Suter	D	2012–present	Led NHL in minutes played per game in 2013

By the Numbers

TOP GOAL SCORER	**Marian Gaborik** 2000–2009 219 goals
TOP GOALTENDER	**Niklas Backstrom** 2006–present 189 wins →
TOP ASSISTS MAN	**Mikko Koivu** 2005–present 322 assists
TOP DEFENSEMAN	**Brent Burns** 2003–2011 183 points

Playoff Run

In just its third season in the NHL, the Wild made a playoff charge all the way to the Western Conference finals. The unlikely run included overtime victories in Games 6 and 7 against the favored Colorado Avalanche. Andrew Brunette's series-winning goal not only led his team to the second round, it also ended the career of goaltending great Patrick Roy, who retired after the season.

Popular Pair

The Minnesota Wild set off fireworks in the hockey world when they signed two of the NHL's biggest stars to long-term contracts July 4, 2012. Forward Zach Parise and defenseman Ryan Suter instantly brought dreams of winning a Stanley Cup to Wild fans. Parise's dad, J.P., played nine seasons for the Minnesota North Stars and was a two-time All-Star.

Zach Parise joined the Wild in 2012.

MONTREAL CANADIENS

First Season: 1917–1918

Franchise Record: 3,210–2,094–837–109
Home Rink: Bell Centre
(21,273 capacity) in Montreal, Quebec, Canada

STANLEY CUPS

1916, 1924, 1930, 1931, 1944, 1946, 1953, 1956, 1957, 1958, 1959, 1960, 1965, 1966, 1968, 1969, 1971, 1973, 1976, 1977, 1978, 1979, 1986, 1993

When it comes to winning, few sports teams have had the success of the Montreal Canadiens. With 24 Stanley Cup victories, only Major League Baseball's New York Yankees have won more championships (27). Twice, the nearly century-old hockey club won four titles in a row, a feat accomplished just one other time in NHL history.

2013 Norris Trophy winner P.K. Subban

Jacques Plante

Jean Beliveau	C	1950–1951, 1952–1971	Won 10 Stanley Cups, including five as team captain
Hector "Toe" Blake		1955–1968	Montreal coach led Canadiens to eight championships
Scotty Bowman		1971–1979	Canadiens coach won five of his nine Stanley Cups with Montreal
Ken Dryden	G	1970–1979	Won the Calder and Conn Smythe trophies as a rookie
Doug Harvey	D	1947–1961	Seven-time Norris Trophy winner
Guy Lafleur	RW	1971–1985	Led the league in scoring three times; won five Cups
Howie Morenz	C	1923–1934, 1936–1937	One of the NHL's first stars was a three-time Hart Trophy winner
Jacques Plante	G	1952–1963	Seven-time Vezina Trophy winner was the first goalie to wear a mask
Carey Price	C	2007–present	First-round draft pick was the All-Rookie Team goalie in 2008
Maurice Richard	RW	1942–1960	"Rocket" led the Canadiens to eight Stanley Cup victories
Larry Robinson	D	1972–1989	Conn Smythe Trophy winner in 1976

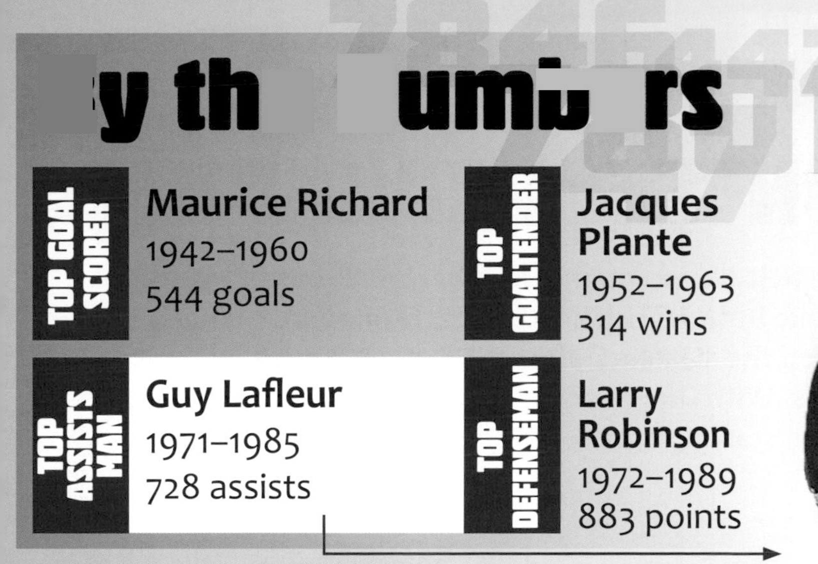

By the Numbers

TOP GOAL SCORER Maurice Richard, 1942–1960, 544 goals	**TOP GOALTENDER** Jacques Plante, 1952–1963, 314 wins
TOP ASSISTS MAN Guy Lafleur, 1971–1985, 728 assists	**TOP DEFENSEMAN** Larry Robinson, 1972–1989, 883 points

Riot for the Rocket

Maurice "Rocket" Richard, a fan favorite, was suspended for the rest of the 1955 season after injuring an opposing player and punching an official. After learning about Richard's suspension, people rioted in the streets of Montreal, causing $500,000 in damage. In 1957 Richard became the NHL's first 500-goal scorer.

Maurice Richard scores against Red Wings goalie Terry Sawchuk during a 1954 game.

The Canadiens' Cup

With 24 championships, the Stanley Cup has belonged to Montreal for nearly a quarter of its history. Jean Beliveau has his name on the Cup 17 times—10 as a player and 7 as a team executive. Henri Richard, brother of Maurice Richard, won it 11 times as a player—more than any other. Yvan Cournoyer also has his name on it 10 times.

1955-1956 MONTREAL CANADIENS

The 1950s saw Montreal dominate the NHL like no team had ever done before. Maurice Richard was a hero to people who spoke both French and English. Forwards such as Bernie "Boom-Boom" Geoffrion, who invented the slapshot, and Jean Beliveau, who led the league in scoring, became fan favorites. With Doug Harvey on defense and Jacques Plante in goal, the Canadiens won five straight Stanley Cups.

The 1955–1956 Canadiens were a great team that featured 12 future Hockey Hall of Fame players, including manager Frank Selke and coach Toe Blake. During the regular season, Beliveau won the scoring title with 47 goals, earning the Art Ross Trophy for leading goal-scorer. He also set a record for most goals and assists as a center. Bert Olmstead, the team's left wing, also set a record with 56 assists.

Toe Blake coached the Canadiens during the 1955–1956 season.

The Canadiens were so talented on the power play that they forced a rule change. Previously, players would serve the full two minutes of their penalty. Montreal scored so often, this rule was changed to end the penalty after a goal was scored against the other team. Richard was at his best, scoring 38 goals. The Canadiens had a fantastic goalie in Jacques "Jake the Snake" Plante. He was the first modern goaltender. He left the net to play the puck and charge shooters instead of waiting for them to shoot. Plante won five straight Vezina trophies as the best goalie in the league and had two shutouts in the 1956 playoffs.

Jean Beliveau (1931-)

Jean Beliveau was among the league's leading scorers for two decades and was team captain during some of the Canadiens' greatest years. He retired after the Canadiens won the Cup in 1971 and became the first player to skate a lap of the ice with the trophy. After his retirement, Beliveau was often urged to run for political office. In 1994 he was asked to become governor general of Canada, which was a great honor. Beliveau said no, out of modesty. In 2003, when Montreal fans booed the U.S. anthem in protest of the war in Iraq, the team played a videotaped message from Beliveau. No one booed after that.

Montreal ended the 1955–1956 regular season with a 24-point lead over the nearest opponent, the second-placed Red Wings. In the semifinals of the playoffs, the Canadiens faced the New York Rangers. The Canadiens won the series 4–1 and advanced to the Stanley Cup finals for the second straight year. In the other semifinal series, Detroit beat Toronto 4–1, setting up a rematch of the previous year's finals.

In Game 1 of the finals, the Red Wings played better for the first two periods. Montreal came back in the third period behind goals from Beliveau, Geoffrion, and Claude Provost and ended up winning 6–4. The Canadiens continued to score a lot of goals in Game 2 and beat Detroit 5–1. Detroit, the defending champions, would not be pushed around, though. In Game 3, behind goals from Red Kelly, Ted Lindsay, and Gordie Howe, the Red Wings won 3–1, bringing the series to 2–1.

The defense of the Canadiens was outstanding in Game 4. Beliveau scored two goals and Floyd Curry added one to lead their team to a 3–0 victory. Montreal was now up 3–1 and was only one victory away from the Stanley Cup. They wanted the championship badly and won the next game 4–1 to take the Cup. Beliveau and Geoffrion continued their great offensive play, each scoring a goal in the game. In the playoffs, Beliveau scored an amazing 12 goals, two being game winners, and had seven assists. He finished the season with a total of 59 goals. The Canadiens were not finished there. They went on to win the Stanley Cup for the next four seasons, stretching out their championship run to five years!

HISTORY BOX

CARRYING THE FLAG

English-speaking colonists and immigrants settled most of Canada, but the French settled the area that is now Quebec. Quebec is very proud of its language and traditions, and the Canadiens are extremely popular there. The team is fondly known as "The Habs," short for "Les Habitants." This is a French term meaning "the country boys" or "the local boys." Local players such as Richard, Beliveau, and Guy Lafleur are heroes there to this day.

1955-1956 Record

Won	Lost	Tied	Playoffs
45	15	10	Defeated New York Rangers 4–1
			Defeated Detroit Red Wings 4–1

The Montreal Canadiens' coach is hoisted into the air to celebrate their victory over the Red Wings.

1976-1977 MONTREAL CANADIENS

The greatest dynasty the hockey world has known was the Montreal Canadiens of the mid- to late 1960s and 1970s. The team truly earned their nickname—"Les Glorieux," or "The Glorious." The Canadiens won 10 Cups in 15 years.

Montreal's best team was the 1976–1977 squad that won the Stanley Cup that season. They won a league high of 60 games and had only eight losses! The way the Canadiens played changed the game. They scored a lot of goals, but concentrated on defense. The Canadiens had nine future Hall of Famers on the roster: Ken Dryden in goal, with Guy Lapointe, Larry Robinson, and Serge Savard on defense. Jacques Lemaire and Bob Gainey were center or played center, and Guy Lafleur, Yvan Cournoyer, and Steve Schutt were on the wings. Sam Pollack was the general manager, and Scotty Bowman was the coach. Both Pollack and Bowman are also in the Hall of Fame.

Ken Dryden (1947-)

In 1971 Canadiens coach Scotty Bowman picked a rookie goalie named Ken Dryden as his playoff starter. Dryden had played in only six NHL games, but the Canadiens won the Cup. Dryden was named Rookie of the Year the next season. Dryden was more than a goalie. He sat out the 1973–1974 season to attend law school. He also wrote a book called *The Game*, which is considered one of the finest books about hockey. Dryden's hockey career was short, but brilliant. In eight seasons he won the Vezina Trophy as best goalie five times, the Conn Smythe Trophy as playoff MVP twice, and played on six Stanley Cup–winning teams.

Lafleur led the league in scoring with 136 points, and Schutt led the league in goals with 60, a record for a left wing. The Canadiens had 132 points in 80 games—a record that hasn't been broken. They lost only once at their home arena, the Forum. This defeat was to the Bruins, early in the year. However, the Canadiens got a chance for revenge in the Stanley Cup finals.

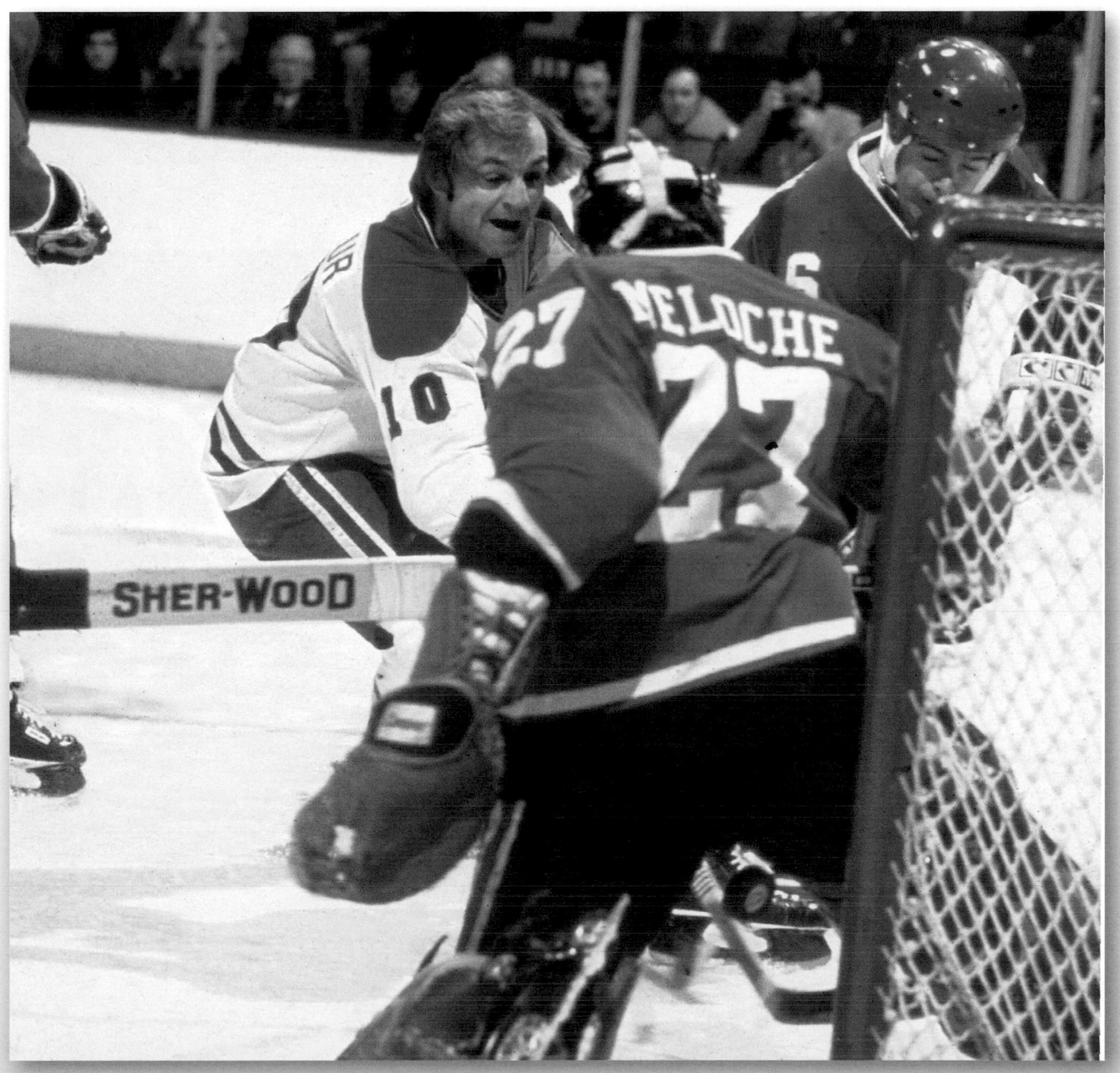

Montreal's Guy Lafleur (center, in white) battles for the puck against the Cleveland Barons.

The Canadiens were just as dominant in the first two rounds of the playoffs as they were in the regular season. They swept St. Louis and beat the Islanders to advance to the Cup finals. They met the Boston Bruins in the championship.

The Canadiens showed that they wanted the championship by scoring two goals in the first five minutes against the Bruins in Game 1. They took only 24 shots all game, but an unbelievable seven of those shots got past Boston's goalie, Gerry Cheevers. The Canadiens dominated and won 7–3. Yvon Lambert and Mario Tremblay each scored two goals for Montreal. As in Game 1, Montreal took very few shots on goal in Game 2. They shot only 19 times, but three shots were for goals. Schutt was Montreal's offensive hero, scoring a goal and assisting on two. Canadiens goalie Dryden blocked all 21 shots he faced, as Montreal shut out the Bruins 3–0. They now held a 2–0 series lead.

Montreal player Serge Savard lifts the Stanley Cup above his head to celebrate the championship.

1976-1977 Record

Won	Lost	Tied	Playoffs
60	8	12	Defeated St. Louis Blues 4–0
			Defeated New York Islanders 4–2
			Defeated Boston Bruins 4–0

In Game 3, the Canadiens continued to dominate. In the first period they took only six shots, but three went in! The Bruins could not stop them, and the Canadiens won 4–2. Facing a sweep in Game 4, the Bruins came out fighting. They got their first lead of the entire series on a goal from Bobby Schmautz, but the Canadiens came right back to tie in the second period. No team scored again, so the game went into overtime. Although it was the best game the Bruins had played all series, they were just no match for Montreal. Four minutes into overtime, Lemaire scored, on an assist from Lafleur, for the game- and Cup-winning goal. The victory gave the Canadiens their 20th Stanley Cup. Lafleur, who led the playoffs in scoring with 26 points, received the Conn Smythe Trophy, given to the most outstanding player in the playoffs.

No team that came before dominated the game the way the Canadiens did. They won an amazing 12 of 14 games in the playoffs. No team that came after had as much pure talent as that team. There would be great players, such as Wayne Gretzky and Mario Lemieux, in the years to come, but no team ever won as easily as the Canadiens did in 1977.

HISTORY BOX

SPENDING TIME WITH THE CUP

Guy Lafleur scored many goals in 1976–1977, but one of the biggest in his career came during the 1979 Stanley Cup finals. He scored late in the third period of Game 7 to tie the game. The Canadiens won the game and the Cup in overtime. While his teammates celebrated that night, Lafleur stole the Cup from the trunk of a car. He showed it off on the lawn of his home. He escaped punishment only because of his popularity. Today, every player on the winning team gets to spend a day with the Cup.

NASHVILLE PREDATORS

Franchise Record: 557–479–60–100

Home Rink: Bridgestone Arena (17,113 capacity) in Nashville, Tennessee

STANLEY CUPS

None

First Season: 1998–1999

In 1971 construction workers in downtown Nashville discovered an underground cave. A 9-inch (23-centimeter) fang and a leg bone of a saber-toothed tiger were found in the cave. Nearly 30 years later, the NHL arrived in Tennessee. Instead of naming the new team after Nashville's famous country-music scene, it was called the Predators and the logo became an ancient tiger.

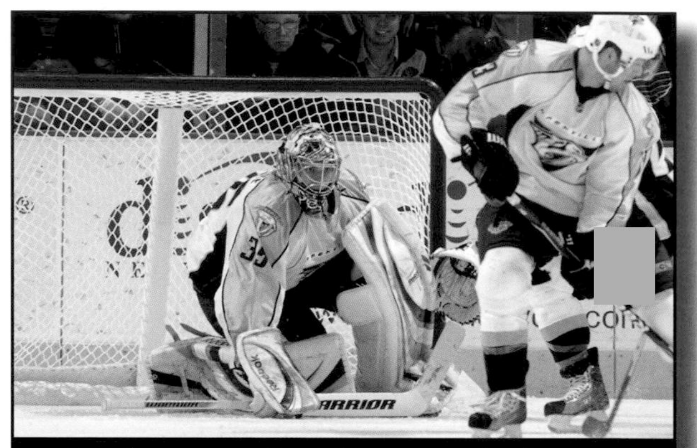

Predators goalie Pekka Rinne had seven shutouts during the 2009–2010 season.

Legends & Stars

Tomas Vokoun

Jason Arnott	C	2006–2010	Went to the All-Star Game in 2008 as a Predator
Steve Sullivan	RW	2004–2011	Bill Masterton Trophy winner in 2009
Tomas Vokoun	G	1998–2007	Named to the All-Star Game twice as a Predator
Shea Weber	D	2005–present	Nashville defenseman is a three-time All-Star

TOP GOAL SCORER	**David Legwand** 1998–2014 210 goals	TOP GOALTENDER	**Pekka Rinne** 2005–present 163 wins
TOP ASSISTS MAN	**David Legwand** 356 assists	TOP DEFENSEMAN	**Shea Weber** 2005–present 347 points

Perfect Marriage

Many expansion teams go through several coaches and managers before getting things right. Not Nashville. For the first 15 seasons of the Predators' existence, general manager David Poile and head coach Barry Trotz ran the team.

Predators coach Barry Trotz (left)

Historic Skate

On opening night of the 2003–2004 season, Predators rookie Jordin Tootoo became the first player of Inuit descent to appear in an NHL game. Tootoo was raised in Rankin Inlet, Nunavut, in northern Canada. Tootoo played five seasons in the NHL, all with Nashville, and had 26 goals and 35 assists.

First Season: 1974–1975

Franchise Record: 1,314–1,361–328–95

Home Rink: Prudential Center (17,625 capacity) in Newark, New Jersey

STANLEY CUPS
1995, 2000, 2003

The Devils started out in the Midwest as the Kansas City Scouts. Two years later, in 1976, they moved west and became the Colorado Rockies. But the team finally found a home on the East Coast in 1982. In New Jersey the team enjoyed its first winning season, its first playoff series win, and three Stanley Cup championships.

Martin Brodeur proudly displays the Stanley Cup after the 2003 FInals.

Patrik Elias

Martin Brodeur	G	1991–2014	Won five Jennings Trophys and four Vezina Trophys
Ken Daneyko	D	1983–2003	Played in a team-record 1,283 games over 20 seasons
Claude Lemieux	F	1990–1995	Conn Smythe Trophy winner in 1995
Zach Parise	LW	2005–2012	High-scoring forward earned an All-Star selection in 2009
Scott Stevens	D	1991–2004	Tough body checker led the Devils to three titles
Patrik Elias	C	1995–present	Three-time All-Star is Devils' all-time leading scorer

TOP GOAL SCORER

Patrik Elias
1995–present
393 goals
590 assists

Patrik Elias
555 assists

TOP GOALTENDER

Martin Brodeur
1991–2014
688 wins

Scott Niedermayer →
1991–2004
476 points

All-Time Winner

In 2009 the Devils' Martin Brodeur won his 552nd game, passing Patrick Roy. The next season, he reached 104 career shutouts and passed Terry Sawchuk's record. But he wasn't done yet. Through the 2013–2014 season, Brodeur had won 688 games and earned 124 shutouts, all with the Devils.

Devils goalie Martin Brodeur

Comeback Kids

To win the 2000 Stanley Cup, the Devils did something no other team had done. They were down three games to one in the conference finals, but they came back to beat the Flyers. They went on to defeat the Stars for the title.

NEW YORK ISLANDERS

First Season: 1972–1973

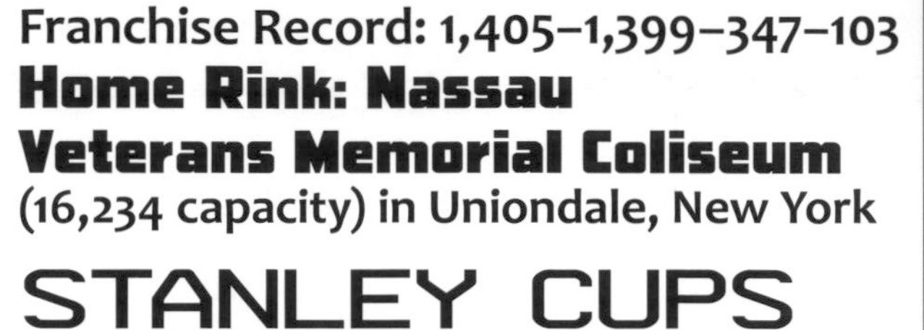

Franchise Record: 1,405–1,399–347–103

Home Rink: Nassau Veterans Memorial Coliseum (16,234 capacity) in Uniondale, New York

STANLEY CUPS

1980, 1981, 1982, 1983

The New York Islanders were the best team of the early 1980s, winning four consecutive Stanley Cups. (Turn the page to learn more about their amazing 1981–1982 season.) Only one other franchise in NHL history had ever accomplished that feat—the Montreal Canadiens did it twice. In 2015 the Islanders will move from Long Island to the New York City borough of Brooklyn.

Four championship banners hang from the rafters in Veterans Memorial Coliseum.

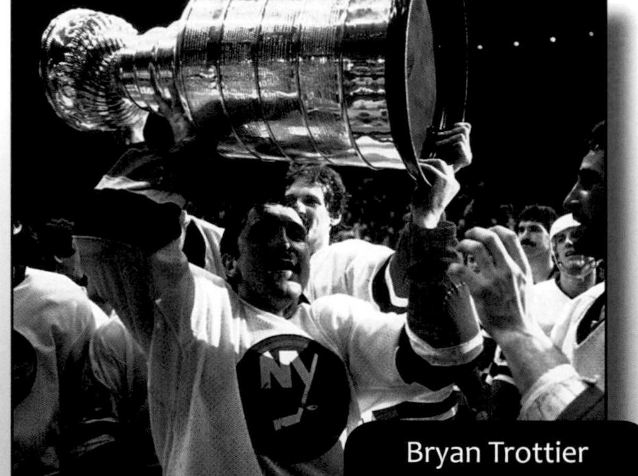

Bryan Trottier

Al Arbour		1973–1986, 1988–1994, 2007	Coached New York's four championship teams
Mike Bossy	RW	1977–1987	Scored a record 53 goals as a rookie
Clark Gillies	LW	1974–1986	Scored 30 or more goals in six different seasons
Denis Potvin	D	1973–1988	Captain of the Islanders' four title teams
Billy Smith	G	1972–1989	Conn Smythe Trophy winner in 1983
John Tavares	C	2009–present	No. 1 overall draft pick in 2009 and 2012 All-Star
Bryan Trottier	C	1975–1990	Retired as the NHL's sixth all-time leading scorer

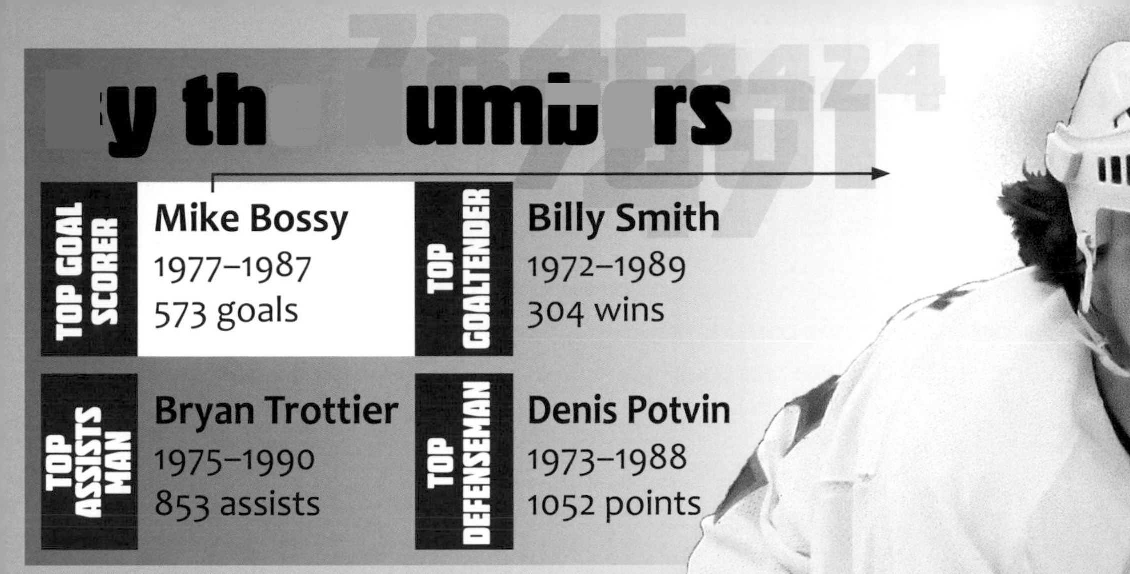

TOP GOAL SCORER	Mike Bossy 1977–1987 573 goals	TOP GOALTENDER	Billy Smith 1972–1989 304 wins
TOP ASSISTS MAN	Bryan Trottier 1975–1990 853 assists	TOP DEFENSEMAN	Denis Potvin 1973–1988 1052 points

Working Overtime

On their way to their first Stanley Cup, the Islanders won six of seven overtime games in the playoffs. That included Game 6 of the finals against the Philadelphia Flyers. Bob Nystrom scored the game-winning goal to give the Islanders the championship.

Bob Nystrom

Easter Epic

In 1987 the Isles won a playoff game that started on a Saturday night in April and didn't end until early Easter Sunday morning. New York's Pat LaFontaine scored during the fourth overtime to clinch the victory. It was the NHL's first four-overtime game in 36 years.

1981-1982 NEW YORK ISLANDERS

Playing on Long Island in the New York City suburbs, the Islanders were a rare team: they were a team without a city. The Islanders' fans considered them New Yorkers at heart, but they had to come from all over Long Island to cheer on their team against the New York Rangers.

The Islanders had powerful forwards such as Bryan Trottier, Mike Bossy, and Clark Gillies, and a great defenseman in Denis Potvin. In the net Billy Smith used his stick to stop pucks and hack at the ankles of any player who got near him. In 1982 the Islanders were at their best, winning their third of four straight Stanley Cups. They led the NHL in wins during the regular season, at one point setting a record with 15 straight wins. The Islanders went into the playoffs as favorites to win the Cup.

Islanders' player Denis Potvin waits for the puck.

However, the first round didn't go as smoothly as they might have liked. They faced a tough Pittsburgh Penguins team. The Islanders started the series strong, winning the first two games. But then they didn't play as well and lost the next two games. The series was tied at 2–2, and it all came down to Game 5. It was a great game. The Islanders were down one goal with only 2:21 remaining when John Tonelli scored a goal and forced overtime. Tonelli continued his heroic play in overtime and scored the game winner, sending his team to the next round.

HISTORY BOX

RIVAL LEAGUES MERGE

After decades in which there were only six pro hockey teams, the 1970s saw the sport change with the NHL's growth to 20 teams. There was also a new league. The World Hockey Association (WHA) was founded in 1972 with 12 teams. Bobby Hull was the first NHL star to sign with the rival association for the then-amazing sum of $1 million! While the NHL had a defensive game, the WHA was all about offense. The WHA collapsed in 1979, and four teams—Edmonton, Hartford, Quebec, and Winnipeg—were invited to join the established league. The Islanders beat Quebec on their way to the Stanley Cup in 1982.

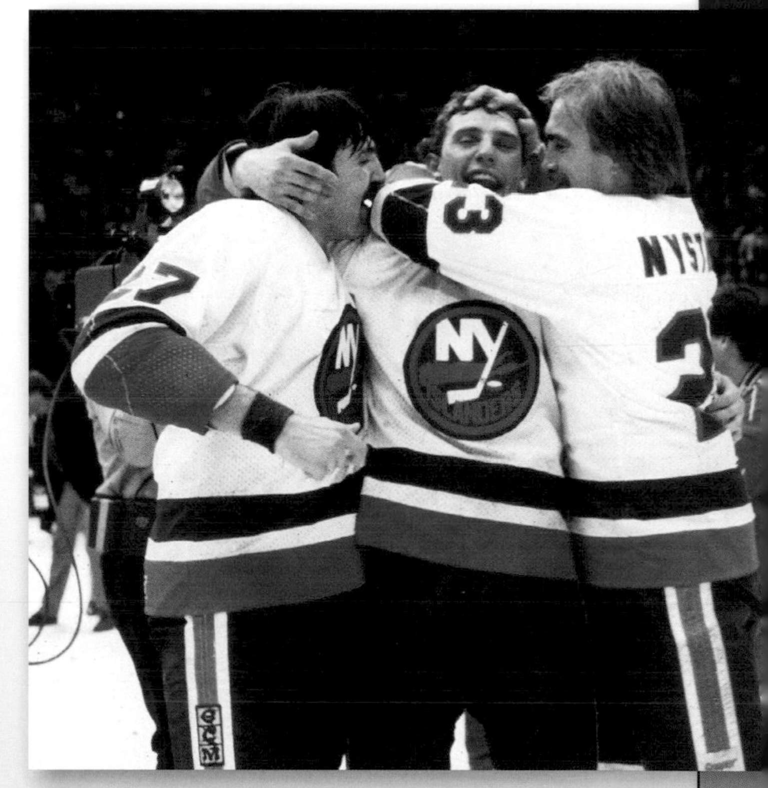

The Islanders won four straight Stanley Cups between 1979 and 1983.

1981–1982 Record

Won	Lost	Tied	Playoffs
54	16	10	Defeated Pittsburgh Penguins 3–2
			Defeated New York Rangers 4–2
			Defeated Quebec Nordiques 4–0
			Defeated Vancouver Canucks 4–0

The Islanders then beat the New York Rangers in six games and swept the Quebec Nordiques to advance to the Stanley Cup finals against the Vancouver Canucks. However, in Game 1, the Canucks played great and led 5–4 with only seven minutes remaining in the game. Their lead didn't last long against the great Islanders. Bossy scored a goal to tie the game at 5–5 with less than five minutes to play. Neither team scored again, and the game went into overtime. Both teams played great defense in overtime, and it looked as if the game would be sent to double overtime. But with only two seconds left, Bossy scored another goal to steal the win. Vancouver came out strong again in Game 2, holding onto a slim 3–2 lead going into the final period. New York came back, scoring two quick goals to take back the lead, 4–3. The Islanders never looked back, scoring two more goals for a 6–4 win and 2–0 series lead.

New York dominated both offensively and defensively in Game 3. They shut out the Canucks, as Gillies, Bob Nystrom, and Bossy all scored goals for a 3–0 victory and 3–0 series lead. The Islanders were only one game away from a sweep and Stanley Cup trophy.

The Canucks didn't want to be swept in the finals, but there wasn't much they could do to stop the Islanders. Bossy proved that he was a great playoff player as he scored two goals in the game. The Canucks never threatened the Islanders as New York won 4–0, earning the Cup and sweeping their opponent. Bossy's 17 post-season goals led to his winning the Conn Smythe Trophy.

Mike Bossy (1957-)

In 1982 Mike Bossy scored one of the most memorable goals in Stanley Cup history. Shoved away from the net by an opposing player, Bossy managed to get his stick on the puck as he fell. With both feet in the air, he fired a backhand into the net. Bossy had a gift for scoring, and it served him well. He is still the only player in NHL history with nine straight 50-goal seasons. Bossy was important for another reason. He didn't like fighting because other players had beat him up when he was young. At the time that Bossy played, fighting was a big part of hockey. Thanks to players like Bossy, the NHL became less violent.

NEW YORK RANGERS

First Season: 1926–1927

Franchise Record: 2,606–2,513–808–97

Home Rink: Madison Square Garden (18,200 capacity) in New York, New York

STANLEY CUPS

1928, 1933, 1940, 1994

The Rangers weren't the first NHL team to play at Madison Square Garden, but they were the survivors. In 1926 the New York Americans also called Manhattan home. But the Rangers, nicknamed the Blueshirts, quickly became the top team in the league. They earned the best record in the league in their first year and clinched the Stanley Cup in their second.

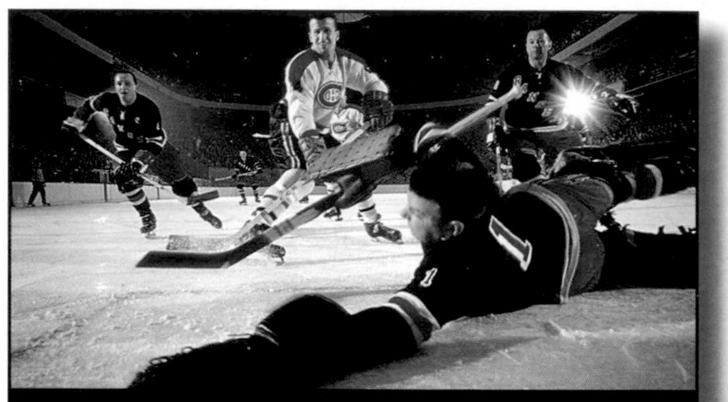

Rangers goalie Gump Worsley was inducted into the Hockey Hall of Fame in 1980.

Henrik Lundqvist

Andy Bathgate	RW	1952–1964	NHL's MVP in 1959
Frank Boucher	C	1926–1938, 1943–1944	Seven-time Lady Byng Trophy winner
Bill Cook	RW	1926–1937	Captain of the Rangers' first two championship teams
Brian Leetch	D	1987–2003	Won two Norris trophies and the Conn Smythe in 1994
Henrik Lundqvist	G	2005–present	Three-time All-Star captured the Vezina Trophy in 2012
Brad Park	D	1968–1975	Named to nine All-Star Games in 17 seasons
Lester Patrick		1926–1939	The Rangers' first coach won two Stanley Cups

By the Numbers

TOP GOAL SCORER

Rod Gilbert
1960–1978
406 goals

TOP GOALTENDER

Henrik Lundqvist
2005–present
301 wins

TOP ASSISTS MAN

Brian Leetch
1987–2003
741 assists

TOP DEFENSEMAN

Brian Leetch →
981 points

1940 Chant

For many years opposing fans mocked the Rangers by chanting "1940! 1940!" during playoff games. That was the last year they had won a title. But captain Mark Messier put an end to the chant in 1994, helping New York hoist the Stanley Cup again. (For more on this Cup-winning season, turn the page.)

Mark Messier was inducted into the NHL Hall of Fame in 2007.

Tex's Team

The Rangers were first organized by Madison Square Garden President G.I. "Tex" Rickard. While the team was being formed, sportswriters had fun with Rickard's nickname. They called the team "Tex's Rangers"—playing off the name of the famous lawmen, the Texas Rangers. Rickard liked the name so much he had it stitched on the team's jerseys.

1993-1994 NEW YORK RANGERS

The New York Rangers were one of hockey's "Original Six." Their last Stanley Cup win came in 1940. In 1993 the Rangers turned to a fiery coach named Mike Keenan. He had taken two teams to the Stanley Cup finals, but players didn't like his harsh methods. The Rangers had talent, but they didn't work very hard as a team. Keenan changed that. He was known for getting his players in shape.

The Rangers didn't even make the playoffs in 1992–1993, but Keenan came in and told his players that his goal for them was to win the Stanley Cup. The players believed that they could do it. Keenan hung a picture of the Stanley Cup in their locker room so that the players would be reminded of what they were playing for.

The Rangers had three great players. Mark Messier was the captain and leader. The Rangers had gotten Messier from the Edmonton Oilers, as well as Adam Graves. Messier had won championships in Edmonton, and his teammates listened to him and respected him, knowing that he could help them win a championship. Brian Leetch was one of the game's best young defensemen, as was rookie Sergei Zubov. The Rangers also had a young goalie named Mike Richter who was ready to become a star. Richter had spent time in the minor leagues the previous year, but he showed he could play at the professional level. He won a league-high 42 games during the regular season!

The Rangers started out the season 4–5. They were very frustrated, and coach Keenan was very angry and disappointed with his team. Keenan motivated his team, and they won 12 out of their next 14 games. They moved into first place and never looked back. They were in first place the rest of the season.

HISTORY BOX

LOCKOUT!

In April 1992, NHL players staged a brief 30-game strike to protest working conditions. That dispute was solved in time for the playoffs. In the fall of 1994, when the agreement expired, NHL owners shut down the league when a new deal couldn't be reached. The season's start was delayed until January, as players wanted more freedom of movement and owners wanted to put a stop to huge increases in salaries. The 105-day lockout couldn't have come at a worse time for the NHL. The Rangers' win captured the attention of both New York and the nation, and hockey was labeled a "hot" sport. The lockout didn't solve much—a decade later, in 2004, and then again in 2012–2013, the owners once again locked out the players.

Mike Keenan (1949-)

Mike Keenan's tough rules brought the best out of his players. He went to the Stanley Cup finals three times with the Blackhawks and Flyers, but he left both teams when he couldn't get along with his bosses. He was in New York less than a month in the fall of 1993 when he smashed a stick on the goal during practice. The Rangers got the message and went on to finish first overall and win the Cup. During the summer, Keenan argued with general manager Neil Smith and jumped to the St. Louis Blues to take on the dual roles of general manager and coach.

1993–1994 Record

Won	Lost	Tied	Playoffs
52	24	8	Defeated New York Islanders 4–0
			Defeated Washington Capitals 4–1
			Defeated New Jersey Devils 4–3

In the first round of the playoffs, the Rangers swept their rivals, the Islanders, outscoring them 22–3. In the second round, they faced the Washington Capitals, beating them four games to one.

In the conference finals, the Rangers met their rivals from across the Hudson River, the New Jersey Devils. The Devils hadn't beaten the Rangers in six regular season games, but it wasn't the regular season anymore. It was a great series full of big goals and big saves. The series had three double-overtime games! The Devils led the series after Game 5, but Messier had something to say. Before Game 6, he guaranteed the Rangers would win. He made sure they did—by scoring a hat trick! The Rangers won Game 7 in double overtime and advanced to the Cup finals.

Rangers captain Mark Messier skates during a game against the New Jersey Devils.

Mark Messier looks for the puck in a game against the Montreal Canadiens.

In the finals, the Vancouver Canucks gave the Rangers everything they could handle. The Rangers started out the series playing great, winning three games and losing only one. The Canucks came back and won Game 5 with a score of 6–3. The Rangers had a chance to win the series in Game 6, but Vancouver won at home 4–1, sending the series back to Madison Square Garden for Game 7. Messier scored to give the Rangers a 3–1 lead, but Vancouver scored in the third period to get within a goal. The Canucks attacked and attacked, but the Rangers held on for their first Stanley Cup in 54 years. In 2004 *The Hockey News* voted it the best Cup final of all time.

OTTAWA SENATORS

First Season: 1992–1993

Franchise Record: 741–699–115–103

Home Rink: Scotiabank Place (20,004 capacity) in Ottawa, Ontario, Canada

STANLEY CUPS

None

For the first 34 years of the 1900s, the Ottawa Senators played professional hockey and even won the Stanley Cup. But the team folded in 1934, leaving Canada's hockey-hungry capital city without an NHL team for almost 60 years. When the league expanded in 1992, a new team with an old name was formed.

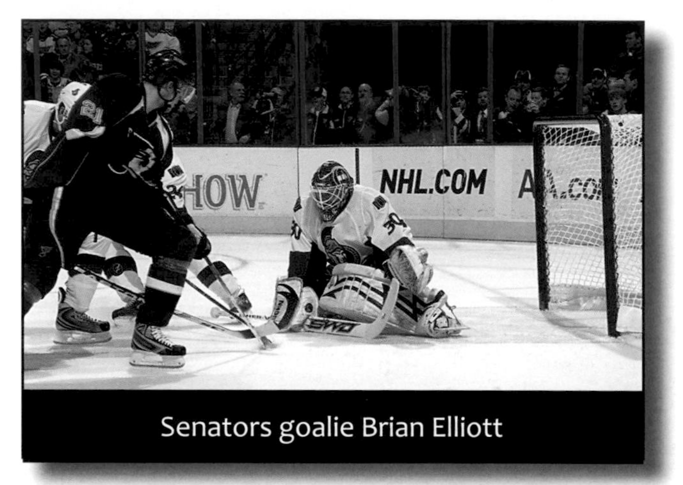

Senators goalie Brian Elliott

Dany Heatley

Player	Position	Years	Note
Craig Anderson	G	2011–present	Led the NHL with a .941 save percentage in 2013
Daniel Alfredsson	RW	1995–2013	Calder Trophy winner in 1996 and six-time All Star
Dany Heatley	LW	2003–2009	Had two 100-point seasons for the Senators
Jason Spezza	C	2002–2014	Drafted second overall in 2001

TOP GOAL SCORER
Daniel Alfredsson
1995–2013
426 goals

TOP GOALTENDER
Patrick Lalime
1999–2004
146 wins

TOP ASSISTS MAN
Daniel Alfredsson
682 assists

TOP DEFENSEMAN
Wade Redden
1996–2008
410 points

Captain Dan

For 17 years, Daniel Alfredsson was the face of the franchise. He was drafted in 1994, joined the team in 1995, and received the captain's "C" in 1999. He also scored the overtime game-winning goal to put Ottawa into the Stanley Cup finals in 2007. They ended up losing the series to the Anaheim Ducks.

Daniel Alfredsson (11)

Tribute to the Past

During their franchise-opening game, the Senators paid tribute to the city's original team. They retired the number 8, the jersey number of Frank Finnigan. He led the old Senators to a 1927 Stanley Cup championship. In his later years, Finnigan campaigned to bring the NHL back to Ottawa.

Philadelphia Flyers

Franchise Record: 1,821–1,254–457–104

Home Rink: Wells Fargo Center
(19,519 capacity) in Philadelphia, Pennsylvania

STANLEY CUPS

1974, 1975

First Season: 1967–1968

In 1967 the NHL expanded from six teams to 12, adding franchises in California, Minnesota, Missouri, and Pennsylvania. One of those Pennsylvania teams, the Philadelphia Flyers, became the first of the new teams to win the Stanley Cup. They won back-to-back titles in their flashy, orange sweaters in the mid-1970s.

The Philadelphia Flyers took on the Boston Bruins in the 2010 NHL Winter Classic.

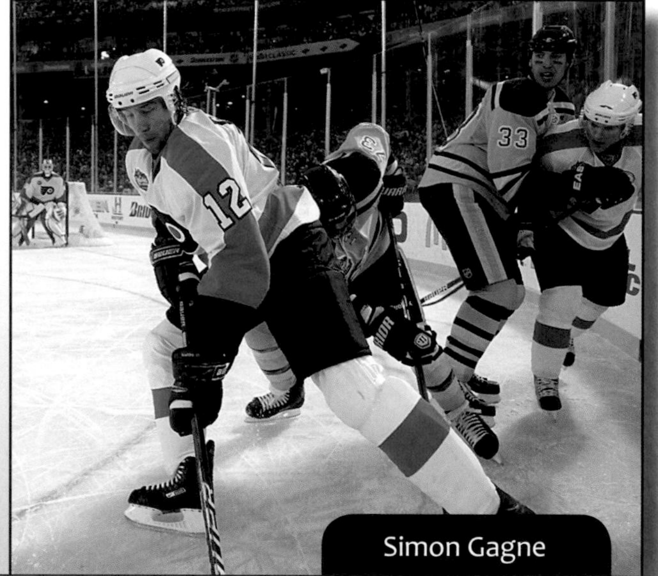

Simon Gagne

Bill Barber	LW	1972–1984	Played in six All-Star Games
Bobby Clarke	C	1969–1984	Three-time Hart Trophy winner
Simon Gagne	LW	1999–2010	All-Rookie in 2000 and two-time All-Star Game pick
Claude Giroux	RW	2007–present	Two-time All-Star collected 93 points in 2011–2012
Eric Lindros	C	1992–2000	Hart Trophy winner in 1995
Bernie Parent	G	1967–1971, 1973–1979	Conn Smythe Trophy winner in each Stanley Cup run
Fred Shero		1971–1978	Coached the Flyers to their two championships

TOP GOAL SCORER	**Bill Barber** 1972–1984 420 goals	TOP GOALTENDER	**Ron Hextall** 1986–1992, 1994–1999 240 wins
TOP ASSISTS MAN	**Bobby Clarke** 1969–1984 852 assists	TOP DEFENSEMAN	**Mark Howe** 1982–1992 480 points

Broad Street Bullies

There wasn't anything fancy about the Flyers' title teams. Captain Bobby Clarke's squad knew how to win ugly games, often intimidating and fighting their opponents. Since their home arena, the Spectrum, was located on Broad Street, the feisty team was given the nickname the Broad Street Bullies.

Flyers left wing Dave Schultz (left) makes a hard check in the 1974 NHL Finals.

Hextall Shoots and Scores

Goaltender Ron Hextall did a lot more than stop pucks. He was considered one of the best puck-handling and passing goalies in the league. On December 8, 1987, Hextall did something no other goaltender had ever done before: shoot and score a goal. It happened late in the game after the Boston Bruins had pulled their goalie for an extra skater. Hextall got the puck and fired it the length of the ice into the empty net. He did it again on April 11, 1989, becoming the first goalie to score in a playoff game.

PITTSBURGH PENGUINS

Franchise Record: 1,594–1,566–383–93

Home Rink: Consol Energy Center
(18,087 capacity) in Pittsburgh, Pennsylvania

STANLEY CUPS
1991, 1992, 2009

First Season: 1967–1968

Few teams get to say they have one of the greatest players of all time in their uniform. For the Pittsburgh Penguins, it was "Super" Mario Lemieux, who led the team to back-to-back championships in the early 1990s. The Penguins are now able to boast of another star: Sidney Crosby. The young phenom took the Penguins to a title in 2009 and scored the game-winning goal for Canada in the 2010 Winter Olympics.

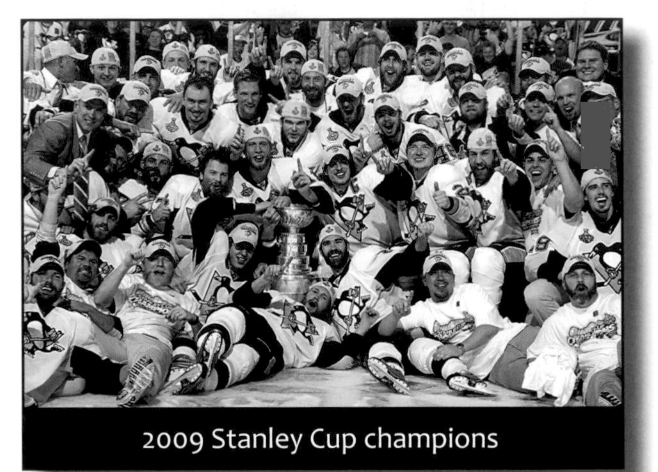
2009 Stanley Cup champions

Jaromir Jagr

Sidney Crosby	C	2005–present	2007 Hart Trophy winner led Penguins to their third Cup
Ron Francis	C	1991–1998	Three-time Lady Byng Trophy winner
Jaromir Jagr	RW	1990–2001	Five-time NHL scoring champion and nine-time All-Star
Mario Lemieux	C	1984–1997, 2000–2006	Three-time Hart Trophy winner; averaged 1.88 points per game
Evgeni Malkin	C	2006–present	Three-time All-Star won the Hart Trophy in 2012

[illegible]

TOP GOAL SCORER	Mario Lemieux 1984–1997, 2000–2006 690 goals	TOP GOALTENDER	Marc-Andre Fleury 2003–present 288 wins
TOP ASSISTS MAN	Mario Lemieux 1,033 assists	TOP DEFENSEMAN	Paul Coffey 1987–1992 440 points

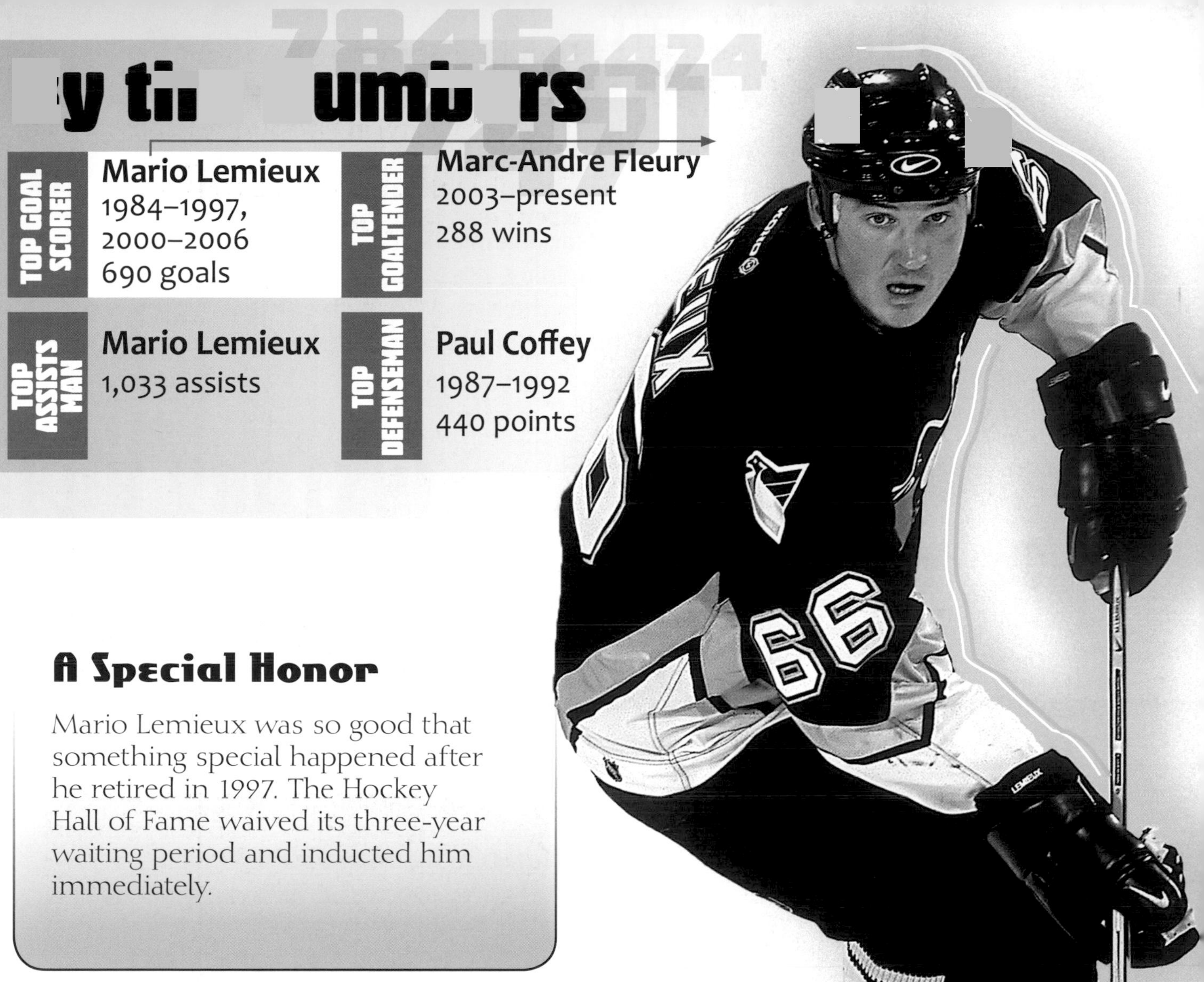

A Special Honor

Mario Lemieux was so good that something special happened after he retired in 1997. The Hockey Hall of Fame waived its three-year waiting period and inducted him immediately.

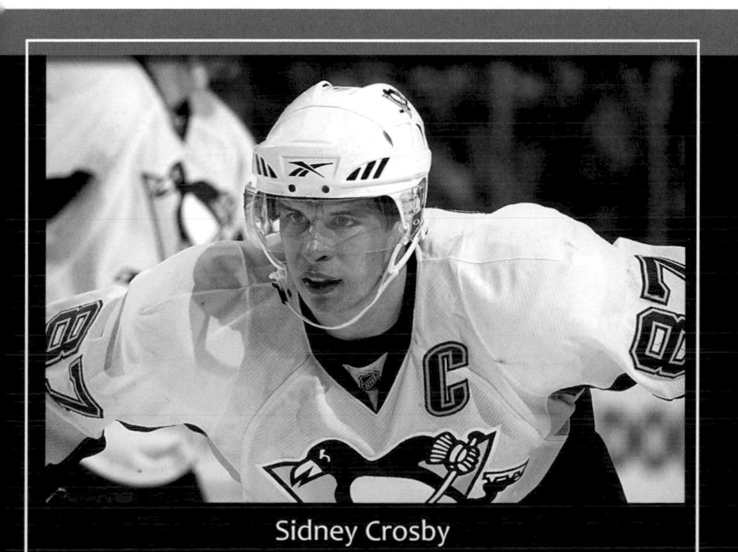

Sidney Crosby

Sid the Kid

Expectations were high for Sidney Crosby when he came into the NHL in 2005, but he more than exceeded them. Crosby became the youngest team captain, the youngest scoring champion, and the youngest player to reach 200 points in league history.

1991-1992 PITTSBURGH PENGUINS

The Penguins were a last-place team when Mario Lemieux arrived in the fall of 1984. But general manager Craig Patrick went about building a team around Lemieux, and by 1992 the Pittsburgh Penguins were the best team in the NHL. With Lemieux leading the way, and stars such as Jaromir Jagr and Ron Francis helping him, the Penguins won back-to-back Cups in 1991 and 1992.

Jaromir Jagr helped the Penguins win the Stanley Cup in 1991 and 1992.

Lemieux was bigger than the great Wayne Gretzky, standing nearly 7 feet tall in skates, but he had the same skills and grasp of the game. Only untimely injuries and illness slowed him down. But it took a long time for Lemieux to become a winner. It wasn't until 1991 that the Penguins were good enough to win the Stanley Cup.

HISTORY BOX

HEAD TO HEAD

There had been other great battles for the scoring title before. Gordie Howe and Maurice Richard spent the 1950s trying to outdo each other. But the hockey world had never seen anything like the scoring race between Mario Lemieux and Wayne Gretzky fought from 1987 to 1994.

Before the 1987 season started, Gretzky had led the league for seven straight years. That year, he played in only 64 games, and Lemieux scored 70 goals to beat out Gretzky for the title, 168 points to 149. Lemieux won the next year as well, with 199 points to Gretzky's 168. The next two seasons, injuries slowed Lemieux, and Gretzky reclaimed the title. Lemieux bounced back to win in 1992–1993, and Gretzky won in 1993–1994—his last scoring title. Lemieux won two more, to give him six in his career. Gretzky won 10.

1991-1992 Record

Won	Lost	Tied	Playoffs
39	32	9	Defeated Washington Capitals 4–3
			Defeated New York Rangers 4–2
			Defeated Boston Bruins 4–0

While they were celebrating their 1991 Cup, tragedy struck. Coach "Badger" Bob Johnson was diagnosed with a brain tumor, and he died in November. Rallying around the memory of their lost coach, and behind new coach Scotty Bowman, the Penguins finished third in their division. They were ready for the playoffs and their chance to defend their title.

In the playoffs, Pittsburgh beat the Washington Capitals, New York Rangers, and Boston Bruins to advance to the finals. Pittsburgh met the Chicago Blackhawks in the Stanley Cup finals. The Blackhawks had been unstoppable early in the playoffs, winning 11 straight games. Instead of being worried about how Chicago was playing, the Penguins remembered that they were defending Cup champions and that they were the best team in the league.

Scotty Bowman took over as coach after the death of Bob Johnson.

In Game 1 of the finals, Chicago jumped out to a 3–0 lead. Instead of giving up, the Penguins tried to come back. Phil Bourque scored for Pittsburgh to make it a 3–1 game at the end of the opening period. Chicago scored again in the second, making it a 4–1 game. The Penguins' Lemieux and Rick Tocchet scored late in the second period to bring them within one goal at 4–3. With less than five minutes left in the game, Penguins' star Jagr scored an unbelievable backhand goal, surrounded by three Blackhawk defenders. The game was tied and looked as if it would be heading into overtime. However, with only 13 seconds remaining, Lemieux scored a goal to win the game.

Pittsburgh's Bob Errey scored the first goal of Game 2. Chicago came back in the second period and tied. Lemieux, the Penguins' superstar, took over, scoring two goals to give his team a 3–1 lead. The Penguins' defense then worked extra hard, only allowing Chicago four shots on goal in the last period. They held for a 3–1 win, taking a 2–0 series lead.

Game 3 was a very good defensive game. Penguins' goalie Tom Barrasso stopped all 13 Chicago shots in the first period. Kevin Stevens scored the only goal of the game for Pittsburgh, giving them a 1–0 victory. Facing a sweep, Chicago came out strong in Game 4. They led 3–0 early, but in the third period it was tied at 4–4. Pittsburgh's Stevens and Francis both scored to make it 6–4. Chicago's Jeremy Roenick scored to make it 6–5, but the Blackhawks could not get any closer. Pittsburgh swept the Blackhawks for their second-straight Cup. Lemieux was given the Conn Smythe Trophy, his second year in a row.

More tragedy would keep the Penguins from gaining a third Cup. Lemieux was diagnosed with cancer in January 1993, and though he beat it and returned to the ice that season, he played only 22 games in the next two seasons. Lemieux returned with an excellent individual performance, leading the league in scoring in 1995–1996 and 1996–1997. Sadly, though, he and the Penguins would never again play for the Cup.

Mario Lemieux (1965-)

Mario Lemieux's 199-point season in 1988–1989 and his leadership in the Penguins' two Stanley Cup titles stand out among his greatest moments. But Lemieux will also be remembered for two off-ice achievements that are as important as what he did on the ice.

In 1993 he was diagnosed with Hodgkin's Disease, which is a form of cancer. Two months later, Lemieux was back on the ice, having missed only 23 games. He later took a year off to recover fully. In that time, he found the Mario Lemieux Foundation, which raises money for cancer research.

He also saved the Penguins for the city of Pittsburgh. In 1998 the team went bankrupt and was at risk of moving or folding. The team owed Lemieux more money than it did anyone else, so Lemieux put together an ownership group and bought the team. When he made his comeback in 2000, Lemieux did it as a player and owner.

First Season: 1991–1992

Franchise Record: 797–710–121–110

Home Rink: SAP Center
(17,483 capacity) in San Jose, California

STANLEY CUPS

None

When the NHL expanded in 1967, California's San Francisco Bay Area got a team. But the Oakland Seals (later, the California Golden Seals) lasted just nine years before moving to Ohio and eventually folding. The league tried the West Coast again in the early 1990s. This time the San Jose Sharks stuck.

Joe Pavelski (8)

Evgeni Nabokov

Patrick Marleau	C	1997–present	San Jose made him the second overall draft pick in 1997
Evgeni Nabokov	G	1999–2010	Calder Trophy winner in 2001
Owen Nolan	RW	1995–2003	Five-time All-Star Game selection
Joe Thornton	C	2005–present	NHL's leading scorer and Hart Trophy winner in 2006

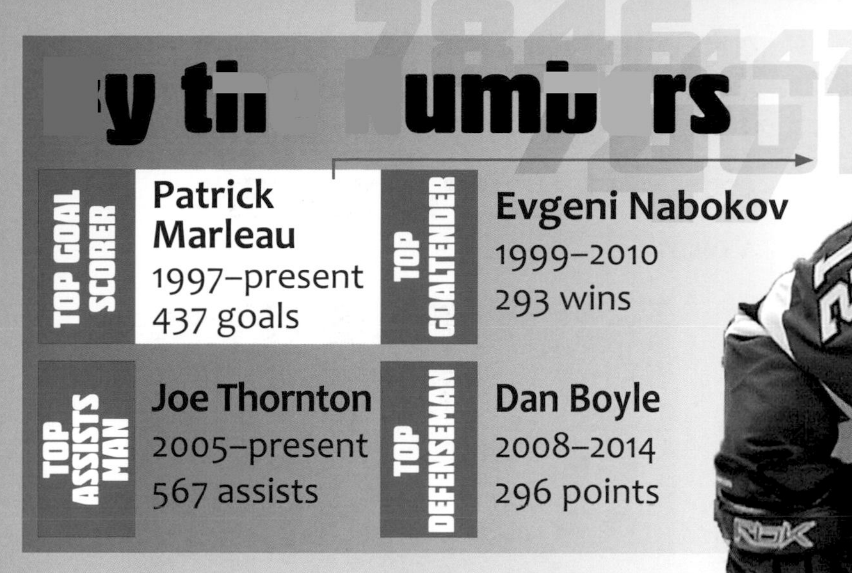

Third Year's a Charm

The Sharks won just 11 games in their second season, but they made a great leap forward in their third year. In 1993–1994 they went from 24 points in the standings to 82. They ended up going 33–35–16 and made the playoffs. But they weren't done there. In the first round, San Jose upset the top-seeded Red Wings in seven games. In the next series, however, the Sharks lost to the Toronto Maple Leafs in seven games.

Big Trade

Early in the 2005–2006 season, the Sharks pulled off a surprising trade when they got center Joe Thornton from the Boston Bruins. Thornton had been the No. 1 overall draft pick in 1997. He had his best season in his first year at San Jose. He led the NHL in scoring and won the Hart Trophy as MVP. With Thornton, the Sharks became one of the top teams, earning the league's best record in 2008–2009.

Joe Thornton (19)

ST. LOUIS BLUES

First Season: 1967–1968

The St. Louis Blues came into the NHL in the late 1960s when the league doubled in size. They immediately went to three Stanley Cup finals. Much of the success came from the aging but future Hall-of-Fame goalies Glenn Hall and Jacques Plante. The Blues remained regular playoff contenders, thanks to stars Brett Hull, Brian Sutter, and Chris Pronger.

Franchise Record: 1,625–1,469–432–110

Home Rink: Scottrade Center (19,260 capacity) in St. Louis, Missouri

STANLEY CUPS

None

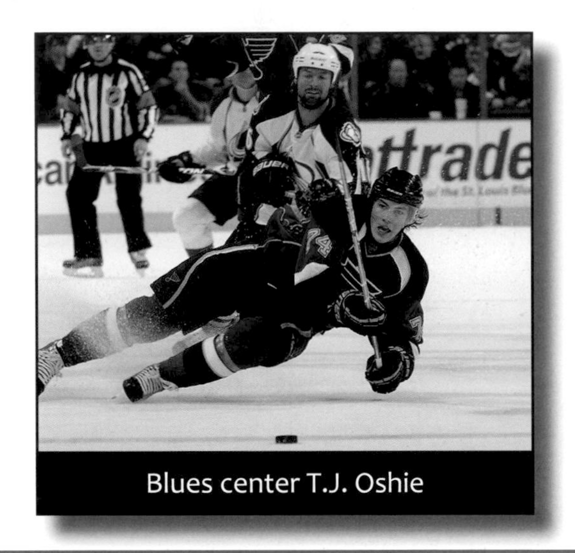

Blues center T.J. Oshie

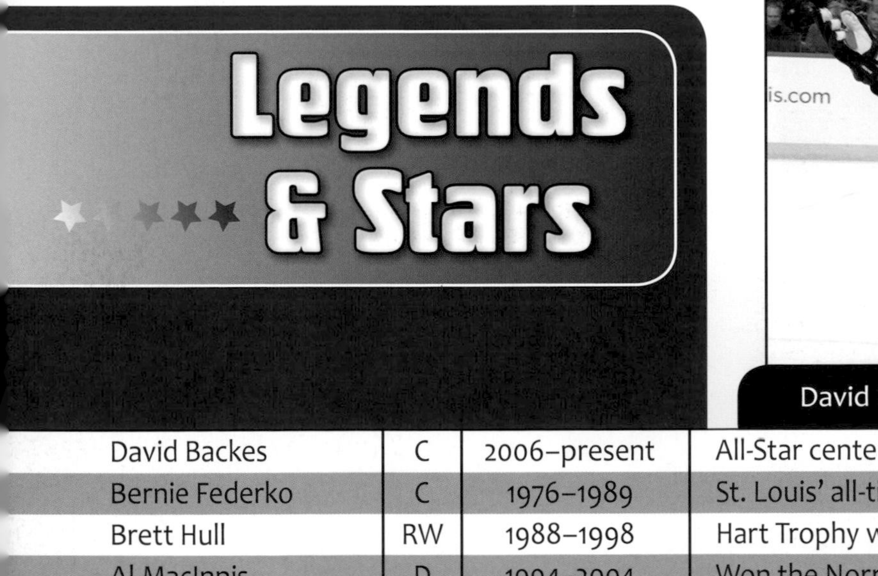

Legends & Stars

David Backes

David Backes	C	2006–present	All-Star center led the team in points in 2011–2012
Bernie Federko	C	1976–1989	St. Louis' all-time leading point scorer
Brett Hull	RW	1988–1998	Hart Trophy winner in 1991
Al MacInnis	D	1994–2004	Won the Norris Trophy in 1999
Chris Pronger	D	1995–2004	First defenseman to win the Hart Trophy since Bobby Orr
Brian Sutter	LW	1976–1988	Three-time All-Star played 12 seasons with the Blues

By the Numbers

TOP GOAL SCORER
Brett Hull
1988–1998
527 goals

TOP GOALTENDER
Mike Liut
1979–1985
151 wins

TOP ASSISTS MAN
Bernie Federko
1976–1989
721 assists

TOP DEFENSEMAN
Al MacInnis
1994–2004
452 points

Comeback Kids

Two of the best games in Blues history were come-from-behind, 6-5 overtime wins. In 1986 St. Louis pulled off "The Monday Night Miracle," erasing a 5-2 third-period deficit to force a Game 7 in the conference semifinals. In a 2000 regular-season game, the Blues were down 5-0 in the third period and came back to beat the Maple Leafs.

A Stop for "The Great One"

Wayne Gretzky is known as the greatest hockey player of all time. He made his career with the Oilers and the Kings. But he also had a short stint with the Blues, finishing the 1995–1996 season in St. Louis. Gretzky scored 21 points in 18 regular-season games and 16 points in 13 playoff games. But the next season, "The Great One" signed with the New York Rangers and finished his career there.

Wayne Gretzky scores his first goal after being traded to the St. Louis Blues.

TAMPA BAY LIGHTNING

First Season: 1992–1993

Franchise Record: 652–785–112–109

Home Rink: Tampa Bay Times Forum (19,758 capacity) in Tampa, Florida

STANLEY CUP

2004

In 1992 the NHL added two new teams. It put one in the heart of hockey country, Ottawa, which had a team in the league until the 1930s. It put the other along the Gulf Coast of Florida and called it the Tampa Bay Lightning. But the Lightning hasn't played like an outsider. The team has been to the playoffs five times and became the southernmost team in the league to win a championship.

Lightning center Steven Stamkos tied the league lead in goals (51) in 2009–2010.

Legends & Stars

Martin St. Louis

Vincent Lecavalier	C	1998–2013	Four-time All-Star led NHL in goals in 2007
Brad Richards	C	2000–2008	Won Conn Smythe and Lady Byng trophies in 2004
Martin St. Louis	RW	2000–2014	Led NHL in scoring and was Hart Trophy winner in 2004
Steven Stamkos	C	2008–2014	Top draft pick in 2008 led the NHL in goals twice

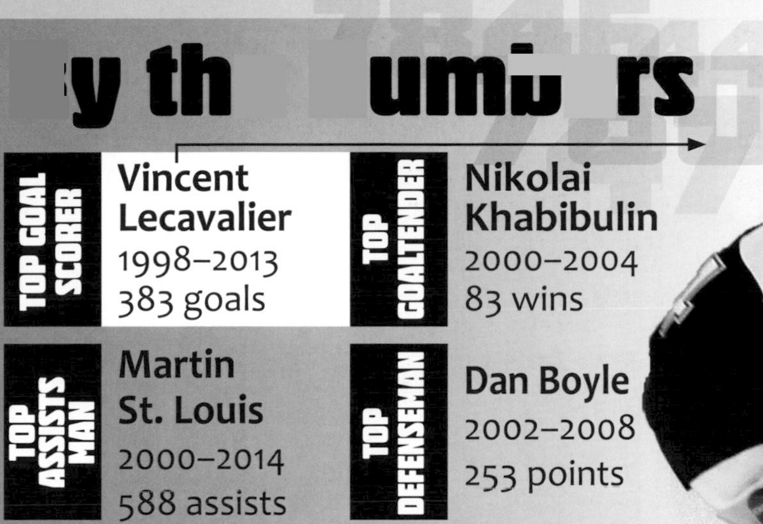

TOP GOAL SCORER	Vincent Lecavalier 1998–2013 383 goals	TOP GOALTENDER	Nikolai Khabibulin 2000–2004 83 wins
TOP ASSISTS MAN	Martin St. Louis 2000–2014 588 assists	TOP DEFENSEMAN	Dan Boyle 2002–2008 253 points

Magical Season

The Lightning had many heroes on their way to winning the Stanley Cup in 2004. Goalie Nikolai Khabibulin had five shutouts and Brad Richards scored 12 goals in the playoffs. League MVP Martin St. Louis scored a double-overtime goal in Game 6 of the finals. Ruslan Fedotenko scored both Tampa Bay goals in the Game 7 clincher.

2004 Stanley Cup champions

Famous First

In 1992 the Lightning made history when they signed goaltender Manon Rheaume. She was the first and only woman to play in the NHL. However, her only appearance came during an exhibition game.

TORONTO MAPLE LEAFS

First Season: 1917–1918

Franchise Record: 2,735–2,623–783–109

Home Rink: Air Canada Centre (18,800 capacity) in Toronto, Ontario, Canada

STANLEY CUPS

1918, 1922, 1932, 1942, 1945, 1947, 1948, 1949, 1951, 1962, 1963, 1964, 1967

Toronto's NHL team was first known as the Arenas. They won a Stanley Cup under that nickname and another as the St. Pats before the legendary Conn Smythe took over the team in the 1920s. He changed the name to the Maple Leafs, after Canada's Maple Leaf Regiment that fought in World War I. Toronto captured 11 titles after the name change. The team has not reached the finals since winning the Cup in 1967.

Maple Leafs center Nik Antropov (11) played more than eight seasons with Toronto.

Tomas Kaberle

Name	Pos.	Years	Notes
Syl Apps	C	1936–1943, 1945–1948	Led Toronto to three titles in the 1940s
Turk Broda	G	1936–1952	Two-time Vezina Trophy winner and five-time Cup winner
Hap Day		1940–1950	Toronto coach led the Leafs to five championships
Tim Horton	D	1949–1970	Seven-time All-Star Game participant
Punch Imlach		1958–1969, 1979–1980	Leafs' coach won four Cups, including a "three-peat" in the 1960s
Tomas Kaberle	D	1998–2011	Selected to the All-Star Game four times
Ted Kennedy	C	1942–1955, 1956–1957	Won the Hart Trophy in 1955
Dave Keon	C	1960–1975	Eight-time All-Star won the Conn Smythe Trophy in 1967
Phil Kessel	C	2009–present	Two-time All-Star led the team in points five straight years
Frank Mahovlich	LW	1956–1968	"The Big M" led the Leafs to four Stanley Cup wins

More Hall of Famers

Of the more than 350 people inducted in the Hockey Hall of Fame, more than 50 have been part of the Maple Leafs organization. That's more than any other team in the NHL. Fittingly, the Hall of Fame is located in Toronto—Canada's largest city.

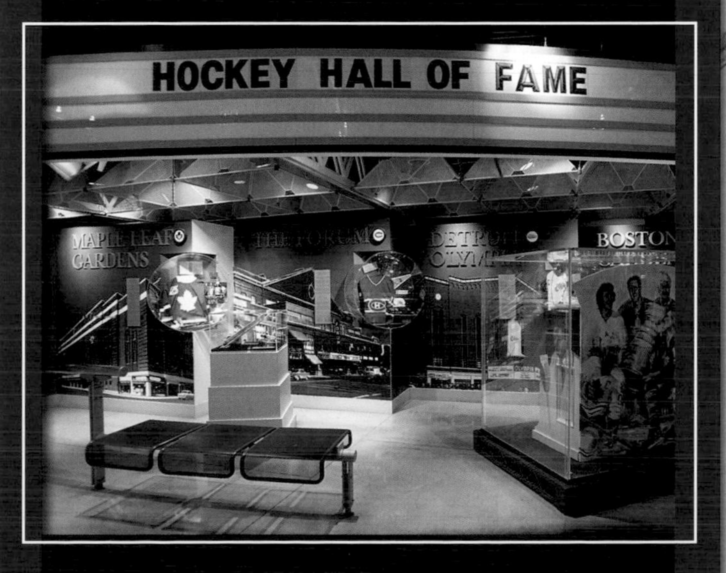

Playing Hurt

Bob Baun might not be one of the Maple Leafs' greatest players, but he sure is a legend. In Game 6 of the 1964 Stanley Cup finals, a puck was shot and hit Baun, breaking his foot. He was taken off the ice on a stretcher, but he returned for overtime. With his foot numbed and taped, Baun scored the game-winning goal. Two nights later, Toronto won Game 7 and their third-straight Stanley Cup.

1966-1967 TORONTO MAPLE LEAFS

Few teams are remembered as fondly in their home city as the 1966–1967 Toronto Maple Leafs. It was the last season for many of the team's popular players, who were getting ready to retire. The goalies were 42-year-old Johnny Bower and 37-year-old Terry Sawchuck. Three key players—Red Kelly, Bob Pulford, and George "Chief" Armstrong—were all 39 years old. Coach Punch Imlach had to take time off to rest during the season. However, the Maple Leafs finished third and faced the league's best team, the Chicago Blackhawks, in the semifinals. Bower was injured during Game 5, and Sawchuck took his place. Sawchuck had 49 saves in 40 minutes as the Maple Leafs won and moved on to the finals against the Montreal Canadiens.

Two Canadian teams would battle for the championship. The Maple Leafs and Canadiens had been the champions in 18 of the past 24 seasons, so it was no surprise to find them facing each other. The Canadiens entered the final series on a 15-game unbeaten streak. In Game 1 Sawchuck started in goal for the Maple Leafs and couldn't stop the Canadiens as they scored four goals against him. The Canadiens rolled to a 6–2 victory. Coach Imlach wasn't pleased with Sawchuck's performance and started Bower in goal for Game 2. It was a good decision. Bower stopped all 31 shots he faced, and the Maple Leafs won 3–0 behind goals from Pete Stemkowski, Mike Walton, and Tim Horton. The series was tied at 1–1.

Terry Sawchuck watches as the Canadiens threaten to score in Game 1 of the Stanley Cup.

Game 3 was a great defensive game by both goalies. Bower faced 63 shots on goal and gave up only two. The game stretched into overtime, and then it went into double overtime. Toronto's Pulford scored the game-winning goal. Before Game 4, Bower hurt his leg, and

1966-1967 Record

Won	Lost	Tied	Playoffs
32	27	11	Defeated Chicago Blackhawks 4–2
			Defeated Montreal Canadiens 4–2

the Maple Leafs were forced to start Sawchuck, who once again could not stop the Canadiens. He allowed six goals, which gave Montreal a 6–2 victory. The series was tied again, at 2–2.

Surprisingly, Sawchuck started Game 5. This time, however, he was ready to play. The first two periods of the game, he dove all over the ice, stopping every shot that came near him. Toronto scored three goals in the second period and broke the game open. In the third period, Toronto's defense was great, as they made it hard for the Canadiens to shoot and pass near their goal. They held on to win 4–1, coming within one win of the Stanley Cup.

Dave Koen attacks the goal during the 1967 Stanley Cup finals.

Coach Imlach stuck with Sawchuck for Game 6, and the goalie stopped all 17 first period shots against him. Ron Ellis and Jim Pappin scored in the second period, giving the Maple Leafs a 2–0 lead. The Canadiens came back and scored a goal, making it 2–1. In the final minute, with the Canadiens threatening to score, a face-off was called in Toronto's zone. Coach Imlach made a daring move and sent in an all-veteran lineup. Once again, his coaching proved to be great, and Allan Stanley, age 41, won the face-off against Montreal's star Jean Beliveau. George Armstrong broke away for a goal, and the Leafs clinched a 3–1 victory. This made them champions for the fourth time in six years. It was their 13th Stanley Cup.

VANCOUVER CANUCKS

First Season: 1970–1971

Franchise Record: 1,415–1,504–391–100

Home Rink: Rogers Arena
(18,630 capacity) in Vancouver, British Columbia, Canada

STANLEY CUPS

None

It took many years for the NHL to arrive in Vancouver, British Columbia. However, Canada's third-largest city had a long history with professional hockey before 1970. In 1915 a team called the Vancouver Millionaires played in the Pacific Coast Hockey Association. The Millionaires even won the Stanley Cup. As for the Canucks, they are still waiting to win their first championship.

Canucks center Ryan Kesler in the 2009 NHL playoffs

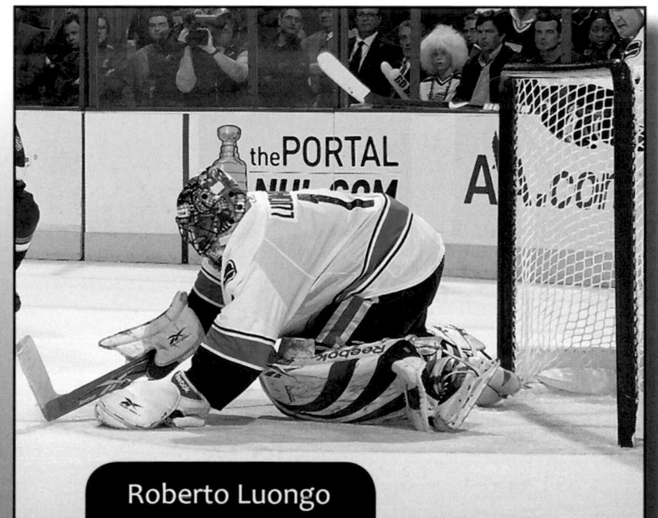

Roberto Luongo

Trevor Linden	RW	1988–1998, 2001–2008	Two-time All-Star Game selection
Roberto Luongo	G	2006–2014	Played in three All-Star Games
Markus Naslund	LW	1996–2008	Won the Lester B. Pearson Award in 2003
Daniel Sedin	LW	2000–present	Two-time All-Star led the NHL in points in 2010–2011
Henrik Sedin	C	2000–present	2010 league MVP is Vancouver's all-time points leader
Stan Smyl	RW	1978–1991	Was the Canucks' leading scorer upon retiring after 13 seasons

Working Overtime

During the Canucks' run to the 1994 Stanley Cup finals, they won seven overtime games. In the first round Vancouver trailed the Flames three games to one before winning three straight overtime games. Star forward Pavel Bure scored the double-overtime goal in Game 7 to send the Canucks to the championship series.

Twin Engines

In 1999 the Canucks made a trade to secure the second- and third-overall selections in the NHL draft. They used those picks to draft twin brothers Daniel and Henrik Sedin. The two have played on the same line together ever since. In 2009 they each signed a new contract to stay in Vancouver—and stay together. The twins are the franchise's top two scorers, both compiling more than 800 career points.

Daniel Sedin (22) and Henrik Sedin (33)

Washington Capitals

First Season: 1974–1975

Franchise Record: 1,370–1,317–303–108

Home Rink: Verizon Center (18,277 capacity) in Washington, D.C.

STANLEY CUPS

None

With such players as Alex Ovechkin and Nicklas Backstrom, the Washington Capitals are one of the most exciting teams in the NHL. It wasn't always that way though. They won just eight games in their first season. At one point they lost 17 games in a row. But since cracking the playoffs in the early 1980s, they've seldom been left out of the postseason.

Capitals goalie Semyon Varlamov defends the net during the 2009 playoffs.

Nicklas Backstrom

Nicklas Backstrom	C	2007–present	2008 All-Rookie selection
Peter Bondra	RW	1990–2004	Five-time All-Star Game pick
Mike Gartner	RW	1979–1989	Seven-time All-Star Game selection
Dale Hunter	C	1987–1999	Ranks second all-time in penalty minutes
Rod Langway	D	1982–1993	Six-time All-Star Game pick and two-time Norris Trophy winner
Alex Ovechkin	LW	2005–present	Won Hart Trophy as MVP in 2008, 2009, and 2013

TOP GOAL SCORER	Peter Bondra 1990–2004 472 goals	TOP GOALTENDER	Olaf Kolzig 1989–2008 301 wins
TOP ASSISTS MAN	Michal Pivonka 1986–1999 418 assists	TOP DEFENSEMAN	Calle Johansson 1989–2003 474 points

Alexander the Great

During his Calder Trophy-winning season, Alex Ovechkin scored what Capitals fans refer to as simply "the goal." Falling on the ice with his back to the goal and his hands above his head, the superstar still found a way to shoot the puck and put it in the net. Two years later, in 2008, Ovechkin became the first player to win the Hart, Ross, Pearson, and Richard trophies all in the same season.

Ironman Streak

Doug Jarvis started his career with the Montreal Canadiens in 1975 and ended it with the Hartford Whalers in 1987. In between he spent four seasons with the Capitals. Along the way, Jarvis never missed a game and set the NHL's consecutive-game streak of 964.

WINNIPEG JETS

First Season: 1999–2000

The Winnipeg Jets began life south of the border as the Atlanta Thrashers. After 11 seasons in Georgia, the team headed north in 2012 and became the Winnipeg Jets. The Jets take their name from Winnipeg's original NHL team, which moved to Arizona in 1996 to become the Coyotes.

Franchise Record: 440–528–45–101

Home Rink: MTS Centre
(15,004 capacity) in Winnipeg, Manitoba, Canada

STANLEY CUPS

None

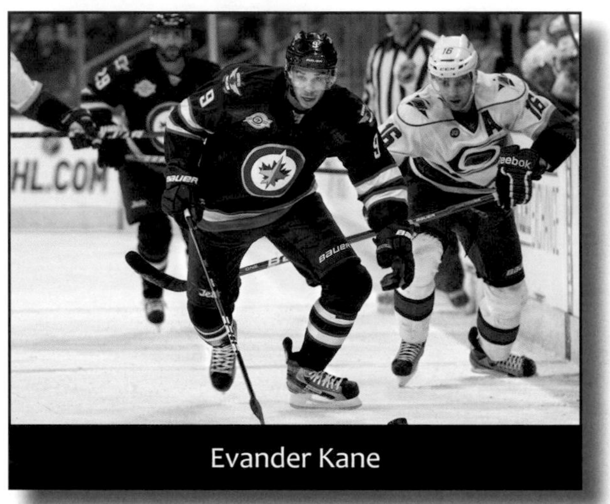

Evander Kane

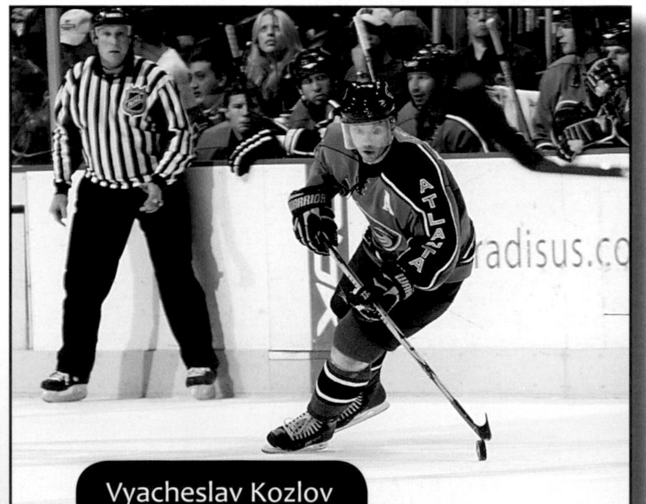

Vyacheslav Kozlov

Evander Kane	LW	2009–present	Selected fourth overall in the 2009 NHL draft
Ilya Kovalchuk	LW	2001–2010	No. 1 overall draft pick in 2001 led the team in scoring and assists
Vyacheslav Kozlov	LW	2002–2010	Longtime Red Wings star had eight game-winning goals during the 2006–2007 season
Kari Lehtonen	G	2003–2009	Led the team in career shutouts with 14

TOP GOAL SCORER

Ilya Kovalchuk
2001–2010
328 goals

TOP ASSISTS MAN

Ilya Kovalchuk
287 assists

TOP GOALTENDER

Ondrej Pavelec
2007–present
113 wins

TOP DEFENSEMAN

Tobias Enstrom
2007–present
249 points

Searching for Success

The Jets have made the playoffs just once in their 14-year history. Led by 100-point scorer Marian Hossa, they went as the Thrashers in 2007 after winning the Southeast Division. However, they were knocked out in the first round by the New York Rangers.

Marian Hossa

Jets Take Off

When it was announced that the NHL was returning to Winnipeg in 2011, the team had hopes that it could sell 13,000 season tickets. No problem. Fans who had waited 15 years for a team to come back to Manitoba bought up the tickets in just 17 minutes. The Jets keep a season-ticket waiting list of 8,000 fans.

Edmonton Oilers
Calgary Flames
Vancouver Canucks
Winnipe
Jets
Colorado Avalanche
San Jose Sharks
Los Angeles Kings
Anaheim Ducks
Arizona Coyotes
TEAM MAP

Montreal Canadiens
Ottawa Senators
Boston Bruins
Toronto Maple Leafs
Minnesota Wild
Buffalo Sabres
New York Rangers
New York Islanders
Detroit Red Wings
New Jersey Devils
Philadelphia Flyers
Pittsburgh Penguins
Chicago Blackhawks
Washington Capitals
Columbus Blue Jackets
St. Louis Blues
Carolina Hurricanes
Nashville Predators
Dallas Stars
Tampa Bay Lightning
Florida Panthers

1960-2014 STANLEY CUP WINNERS

1960–1961	Chicago Blackhawks
1961–1962	Toronto Maple Leafs
1962–1963	Toronto Maple Leafs
1963–1964	Toronto Maple Leafs
1964–1965	Montreal Canadiens
1965–1966	Montreal Canadiens
1966–1967	Toronto Maple Leafs
1967–1968	Montreal Canadiens
1968–1969	Montreal Canadiens
1969–1970	Boston Bruins
1970–1971	Montreal Canadiens
1971–1972	Boston Bruins
1972–1973	Montreal Canadiens
1973–1974	Philadelphia Flyers
1974–1975	Philadelphia Flyers
1975–1976	Montreal Canadiens
1976–1977	Montreal Canadiens
1977–1978	Montreal Canadiens
1978–1979	Montreal Canadiens
1979–1980	New York Islanders
1980–1981	New York Islanders
1981–1982	New York Islanders
1982–1983	New York Islanders
1983–1984	Edmonton Oilers
1984–1985	Edmonton Oilers
1985–1986	Montreal Canadiens
1986–1987	Edmonton Oilers
1987–1988	Edmonton Oilers

1988–1989	Calgary Flames
1989–1990	Edmonton Oilers
1990–1991	Pittsburgh Penguins
1991–1992	Pittsburgh Penguins
1992–1993	Montreal Canadiens
1993–1994	New York Rangers
1994–1995	New Jersey Devils
1995–1996	Colorado Avalanche
1996–1997	Detroit Red Wings
1997–1998	Detroit Red Wings
1998–1999	Dallas Stars
1999–2000	New Jersey Devils
2000–2001	Colorado Avalanche
2001–2002	Detroit Red Wings
2002–2003	New Jersey Devils
2003–2004	Tampa Bay Lightning
2004–2005	No champion due to lockout
2005–2006	Carolina Hurricanes
2006–2007	Anaheim Ducks
2007–2008	Detroit Red Wings
2008–2009	Pittsburgh Penguins
2009–2010	Chicago Blackhawks
2010–2011	Boston Bruins
2011–2012	Los Angeles Kings
2012–2013	Chicago Blackhawks
2013–2014	Los Angeles Kings

GLOSSARY

assist pass that leads to a goal; as many as two assists can be awarded on one goal

body check when a player uses a hip or shoulder to bump an opponent off the puck

conference grouping in hockey; teams are grouped into two conferences—the Eastern Conference and the Western Conference

dynasty team that wins multiple championships over a period of several years

face-off dropping the puck between two players to restart play

franchise team that operates under the rules and regulations of a professional sports league or organization

hat trick three goals in one game

MVP (Most Valuable Player) hockey award given to the player who helps his or her team the most. In the NHL, the actual award is called the Hart Trophy.

National Hockey League (NHL) professional hockey league that was founded in 1917. As of 2015, there were 30 teams in the NHL.

overtime extra period played if the score is tied at the end of a game

period division in a hockey game; a hockey game is divided into three 20-minute periods

power play when a player serves a penalty, the opposing team has a one-person advantage, usually for two minutes or until the team on the power play scores

rookie first-year player

seed how a team is ranked for the Stanley Cup playoffs, based on the team's regular season record and point total

shootout method of breaking a tie score at the end of overtime play

shutout game in which one team fails to score a goal

Stanley Cup silver trophy awarded to the NHL champions

sweep winning all of the games in a series

veteran older, more experienced player

World Hockey Association (WHA) professional hockey league that was created in 1972 to compete with the NHL. The WHA merged with the NHL in the 1979–1980 season.

HOCKEY POSITIONS

center (C) forward who plays in the middle of the rink

defenseman (D) one of two players who stays by the ice's blue line to help defend his or her goal

goaltender (G) player who plays in front of the net and tries to stop the other team from scoring

left wing (LW) forward who plays on the left side of the rink

right wing (RW) forward who plays on the right side of the rink

NHL AWARD TROPHIES

Art Ross Trophy leading point scorer

Bill Masterton Memorial Trophy player who displays perseverance and dedication to hockey

Calder Memorial Trophy rookie of the year

Conn Smythe Trophy most valuable player of the playoffs

Frank J. Selke Trophy top defensive forward

Hart Memorial Trophy most valuable player

Jack Adams Award coach of the year

James Norris Memorial Trophy top defenseman

King Clancy Memorial Trophy player who displays leadership on the ice and in the community

Lady Byng Memorial Trophy player who displays gentlemanly conduct

Lester B. Pearson Award MVP as voted on by the players

Maurice "Rocket" Richard Trophy leading goal-scorer

Vezina Trophy top goaltender

William M. Jennings Trophy goaltender with the lowest goals-against average

Frederick, Shane. *The Technology of Hockey.* Sports Illustrated Kids. North Mankato, Minn.: Capstone Press, 2013.

Frederick, Shane. *The Ultimate Collection of Pro Hockey Records 2015.* Sports Illustrated Kids. North Mankato, Minn.: Capstone Press, 2014.

Goldner, John. *Hockey Talk: The Language of Hockey from A–Z.* Markham, Ontario: Fitzhenry & Whiteside, 2010.

Weekes, Don. *World Class Trivia.* Vancouver, BC: Greystone Books, 2009.

INTERNET SITES

FactHound offers a safe, fun way to find Internet sites related to this book. All of the sites on FactHound have been researched by our staff.

Here's all you do:

Visit www.facthound.com

Type in this code: 9781491419632

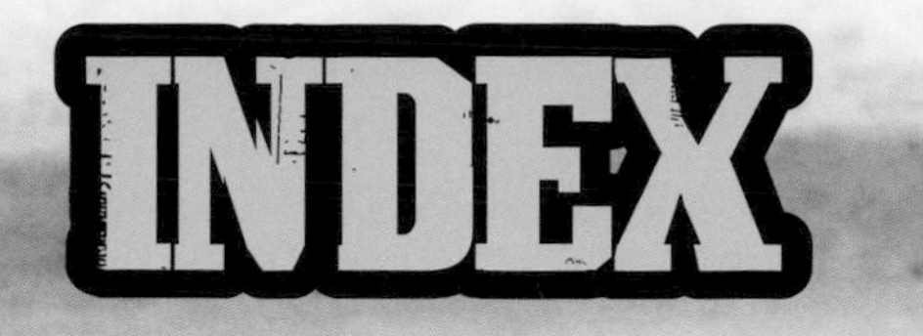
INDEX